THE COMPLETE BOOK OF
SALT BLOCK COOKING

THE COMPLETE BOOK OF
SALT BLOCK
COOKING

Cook Everything You Love with a Himalayan Salt Block

RYAN CHILDS

Photography by Kelly Ishikawa
Styling by Rod Hipskind

SONOMA
PRESS

CONTENTS

INTRODUCTION

As a chef, I tend to rely on the same dozen or so tools regardless of what I am preparing. Rarely a day goes by that I don't reach for a sharp knife and place a pan over a burner. I've never been one to be carried away by the latest kitchen gadget, so the first time I saw a Himalayan salt block, I was skeptical. I thought that it was unique and beautiful but that it would likely be another unused tool collecting dust in an otherwise crowded kitchen. After all, why would I want to cook on a salt block if I already have a frying pan? So, when I received a salt block as a gift, it sat on my kitchen counter propped against a stack of cookbooks as I continued to reach for my familiar kitchen tools.

When I did become motivated to give the salt block a try, I looked for guidance. Finding limited resources, I reviewed a list of do's and don'ts, placed my salt block on the stovetop and ignited the burner. As the block collected heat, it lightened in color, emitted a creak or two as it became increasingly hot, and that was it. There were no fireworks or grand spectacle, just an evenly heated surface waiting to be put to use. I removed a steak from the refrigerator, cracked some pepper on both sides, applied a little oil, and placed it on the salt block. When finished cooking, what sat before me was a beautifully seared steak.

From that moment forward I've become fascinated with using my salt block to prepare the foods I enjoy making with traditional equipment: a seared steak, roasted vegetables, or a fried egg.

The more I cooked with the block, the more it shed its rosy façade, revealing a darker surface that begged to be used. It invited itself to join the ranks of my prized kitchen tools. I used my salt block in place of my pizza stone and watched it show its flexibility and range as I baked cookies, a pear tart, and flatbread. The salt block even worked wonderfully reheating leftovers.

This isn't to suggest that the salt block is a tool that can do anything. Experimentation and curiosity are required. The goal of this book is to teach you how to use a Himalayan salt block to prepare foods you really love in a new way, and to introduce new foods and preparations that lend themselves particularly well to use with a salt block. I've also included recipes that utilize salt bowls and salt cups to encourage exploration. Part One will arm you with salt block cooking basics, and in Part Two you'll find over 100 recipes, as well as must-know tips specific to each chapter.

Salt block cooking is a wonderful reminder that even simple favorites can seem exotic. Enjoy the adventure!

GETTING TO KNOW YOUR SALT BLOCK

CHAPTER ONE

YOUR SALT BLOCK COOKING PRIMER

Cooking with a Himalayan salt block is a unique and delicious endeavor. While a brand-new block may look more like a household decoration than your next go-to kitchen tool, you'll soon discover its versatility and impact. Just as a properly seasoned dish can make the difference between a memorable meal and one that is simply ordinary, preparing food on a Himalayan salt block provides balanced seasoning of the food that cannot be reproduced in another way. Your salt block is versatile. It gives a perfect sear to all kinds of proteins, leaves vegetables wonderfully crisp, and it lends a spectacular hint of salt to baked goods.

The 102 recipes in this book are designed to teach you how to use your salt block to take the foods you love to a whole new level. But first we'll take some time to let you get to know your salt block and unlock its potential. Understanding your block's strengths and quirks will be the key to success. While mastering the art of salt block cooking takes some patience, you'll find that after a bit of experimentation and practice, your trials will be well worthwhile.

METHODS

There are five general methods of using your salt block: stovetop cooking (searing), roasting and baking, grilling, curing, and preparing or presenting. Let's take a closer look at these salt block methods and what they mean for your food.

STOVETOP COOKING

Using the salt block on the stovetop will give your food a perfect sear. A 2-inch-thick salt block retains heat longer and radiates it more evenly than any pan you may have, including cast iron, making it invaluable for stovetop cooking. In order to safely use a salt block on the stovetop, it must be heated gently, which means heating it on low heat for what can be as much as half an hour, depending upon the block's thickness. This extra time is comparable to preheating an oven, so it should not be seen as a drawback. By the time you gather and prep the ingredients in a recipe, the salt block will be ready. Foods seared at a high temperature will develop a beautiful crust, while foods cooked at a lower temperature will benefit from even and gradual radiant heat.

ROASTING AND BAKING

Salt blocks work well in place of a pizza stone or baking sheet. They deliver even heat and cook foods gently. However, it is important to preheat your salt block on the stovetop before placing it in the oven. As a general rule you should try to have your salt block as close as possible to the oven temperature when you place it inside.

GRILLING

There are a number of advantages to using a salt block on the grill. A salt block prevents smaller foods from being lodged in between grill grates or falling through altogether. It also prevents food from being burned by flare-ups. Liquid released from the food tends to run off the salt block onto the hot coals, giving the food a smoky flavor. The density of salt blocks makes them especially useful on gas grills, which are prone to "cool spots," as the salt block allows for even heating. You can also use the salt block as a weight during grilling to introduce heat to the top of foods while the grill heats them from the bottom.

CURING

Using a salt block to cure foods expedites the curing process. As the food releases its liquids it creates a brine, which in turn seasons the food faster. For this reason it is a good idea to place the salt block on a baking sheet when curing so as to catch any runoff liquids.

PREPARING AND PRESENTING

While it might not seem that there is much to using your salt block to prepare and present food, there's a lot of pleasure in the simplicity of this method. Plus, it's sure to be a crowd-pleaser. Food prepared on a hot salt block takes on a gentle and even seasoning of salt. When the salt block is chilled or at room temperature, the food you prepare on it will take on salt faster. For this reason, always serve foods immediately unless otherwise instructed.

YOUR SALT BLOCK'S ORIGINS

Ever wonder where salt blocks come from? Although there are great deposits of salt in the towering Himalayas—most of which are part of India, Nepal, and Bhutan—the extreme and isolated geography makes it difficult to mine, and thus not economically feasible. The salt blocks available to us are mined from the Salt Range hills in neighboring Pakistan, where the geography is much more favorable. Despite their true origins, we still call our salt blocks by the romantic and appealing name "Himalayan," though.

The Salt Range is located in the north of the Punjab region of Pakistan. Unlike the soaring Himalayas, which boast the world's highest mountain (at 29,035 feet), the average height of the hills in the Salt Range is 2,200 feet, with its highest peak, Sakesar, standing at 4,992 feet. This more moderate geography lends itself well to commercial mining.

The Salt Range is home to six primary salt mines, and the methods used to mine salt have changed little since 1827. The "room and pillar" method of mining creates vast underground networks where as much as 350,000 to 400,000 tons of salt are mined annually, mostly by hand. The salt used for salt blocks comes from deep within the seam, presumably where time and

pressure have compacted the densest boulders of salt. Here, miners uncover boulders weighing hundreds of pounds, breaking them apart with hand tools so that they can be hauled out of the mine. Once extracted, these boulders are cut down in size and eventually formed into salt blocks each weighing just a few pounds.

TOO MUCH SALT?

Salt blocks do salt your food, but not as much as you may think. Salt blocks are incredibly dense and their surfaces are flat. This means that there is relatively little contact with the food compared to granular or flaked salts. Surprisingly, foods take on very little salt when cooking at high temperatures. Sometimes I even find myself adding a little more salt to food that I prepared on a salt block.

There are three factors to consider regarding seasoning foods with your block. If you keep these in mind as you experiment in the kitchen, you'll be set up for success.

TEMPERATURE Whereas a very hot salt block transfers very little salt to foods, warm or room temperature blocks will transfer salt to foods rather quickly. This means that dishes prepared on and served from the salt block, such as Salted Lime Guacamole (page 38), must be eaten immediately. Since only the bottom portion of the food is in contact with the salt block, it is important to periodically mix the guacamole as you eat it. I recommend dragging a tortilla chip along the bottom of the salt block to mix the saltier mixture with the less salty portions.

When searing foods, make sure that the salt block is extremely hot before adding food to the block, just as you would with a pan. This is important for two reasons. First, using a fully heated salt block creates a nonstick surface. Second, the hotter the block, the less salt will be transferred to your food. A hot block quickly dries, sealing the outside of your food with a crust, and slowing the transfer of salt.

TIME Simply put, the longer food sits in contact with the salt block, the more salt it will absorb. You must take this into consideration when cooking or serving cooked food on a salt block.

MOISTURE Liquid will dissolve the salt block and transfer salt to your food faster. This is one reason it is important to pat foods dry before placing them on the salt block. Furthermore, if you are searing on the salt block, dryer foods also reduce sticking.

WHAT GIVES SALT BLOCKS THEIR COLOR?

While usually described as pink or rosy, the color of Himalayan salt blocks range a great deal. The color of a salt block is influenced by trace minerals, which were trapped in the salt hundreds of millions of years ago. Potassium, copper, magnesium, iron, and sulfur are locked into the salt crystals, resulting in swirls of white, pink, rose, and brown hues. I like to think of salt blocks like marble: Each piece has its own unique mineral deposits, flaws, imperfections, and beauty.

SHOPPING FOR A SALT BLOCK

Finding a salt block isn't difficult, but finding one that can be used for cooking takes a little more effort. The most important consideration is to buy from a reputable vendor who deals only in high-quality cooking salt blocks. Avoid lesser-quality salt blocks, which are more likely to crack—or, worse, explode—during heating. Buy from a dealer who has direct contact with the supplier. These dealers will often offer a guarantee against breakage, a good sign that you have found a high-quality salt block. There is perhaps no better source than The Meadow, located in Portland, Oregon, and New York City. Mark Bitterman, the owner, has filled his stores with an impressive selection of salt blocks, cups, dishes, and plates along with over a hundred different types of finishing salts. Culinary suppliers like Sur La Table and Williams-Sonoma are also excellent resources for basic salt blocks.

Once you've located your supplier, the next step is determining how you intend to use your salt block. There are two basic types of kitchen salt blocks. The first is a "table grade" or "serving" salt block. This is intended for cooler uses—in other words, it will not be used to cook with. These salt blocks can be used for curing foods and for presentation of uncooked foods like dips and cheeses. These blocks may be a little thinner than salt blocks intended for cooking. The main characteristic of a presentation salt block is its beauty, so the focus is on selecting a salt block based upon its unique color and translucency.

The second type of salt block is one used to prepare food. There are six factors to consider when selecting a salt block for cooking.

SIZE Larger salt blocks, about 9 by 9 inches or bigger, are good for heating foods, while smaller salt blocks are better for serving foods or for using as weights to press or flatten foods during cooking or curing. If you are looking for smaller salt blocks, consider purchasing two same-size ones; use one as a weight for recipes that call for sandwiching foods between blocks, and use the other for presentation. Larger serving blocks are better for eating family style, while smaller blocks can be used for individual servings.

THICKNESS Thicker salt blocks are better for heating and cooking. Remember, though, the thicker the salt block, the longer it will take to heat. A 1½-inch-thick salt block has 25 percent less mass than a 2-inch-thick salt block, so it will require less time and energy to heat. You don't have to have a thick salt block in order to cook on it, but I do recommend that a salt block that will be heated should be at least 1½ inches thick.

QUALITY Just as the thickness of a salt block determines how well it can be heated and cooled, so does its quality. A salt block should be just that—salt. There should be no other materials in it, such as sand. In addition, the block should be very dense, without air pockets or cracks running through it. This is why it is essential to purchase salt blocks only from reputable suppliers who sell blocks intended for cooking. Spend a little more and ask if there is a written guarantee against breakage. The additional use you get out of a higher quality block will be well worth it.

COLOR The color variations you see in salt blocks come from trace minerals like copper, potassium, and iron. They do not affect the quality of the salt block, just its appearance and flavor. Similar to slabs of marble, salt blocks have unique color deposits, flaws, and fissures. But unlike most marble, even thick salt blocks have an intense translucency and seem to glow when light passes them. This is a great reason to shop at a store where you can compare different blocks and select one of unique beauty. Don't be concerned about the color of the salt block you will use to cook with. The constant heating and reheating of a salt block changes its color, initially lightening and eventually darkening it.

SHAPE While most of the recipes in this book rely on a rectangular "slab" salt block, there are other interesting salt block shapes, such as cups and bowls. Cups are fun for serving drinks and cocktails. Bowls can be used to mix and serve salads as well as to marinate foods. Marinating in a salt block bowl slowly draws in the salt from the bowl, while at the same time the bowl traps released liquids and increases the marinating rate of food as the dissolving salt creates a mini brine, which in turn accelerates the rate of seasoning.

QUANTITY I recommend beginning with one salt block, about 12 by 8 by 1½ inches. This will allow you to try it out and discover a few go-to recipes that work well for your cooking style and taste. As you become comfortable cooking with your salt block, you may discover that another shape or size will work better for you. Eventually your salt block will crack and split into pieces. You will find new uses for these pieces, such as grating the salt block over foods to season them or using the broken pieces as weights to press a piece of meat on the grill. Having multiple salt blocks allows you both "workhorse" blocks, which become discolored over time, and pristine serving blocks, which maintain their original colors.

TOOLS OF THE TRADE

Yes, there are plenty of accessories and tools you can buy for your salt block, but you really need only a few. Here is a list of the essential items— odds are that you already have many of these items in your kitchen.

- **SILICONE OVEN MITTS** Salt blocks are dense objects that retain much more heat than even the heaviest cast iron pan. For this reason you must be extremely careful when moving a hot salt block. Silicone mitts are designed to withstand heat up to 600°F. Alternatively, you can use heavy gloves. I strongly advise against using a folded kitchen towel, since I have found that the salt block heat is transferred to the hands very quickly.

- **METAL SPATULA** Any metal spatula will work just fine, but I prefer a spatula with a slightly angled edge. This helps scrape burned material off the salt block and makes cleaning extremely easy. The angled edge also makes it easier to flip items prone to sticking, like eggs and fish.

ENTERTAINING WITH SALT BLOCKS

Salt blocks lend themselves well to entertaining since they can be used to serve a variety of foods. Many of the recipes in this book are intended to be both prepared and served on a salt block. What better way to present Simple Fish Crudo (page 41) or Warm Brie with Fall Fruit (page 87) than on a 2-inch slab of rosy salt? It's rustic and refined at the same time. I find that the simplest preparations are often the most dramatic: Imagine having overnight guests gather in the kitchen for breakfast as you prepare Sunny-Side Up Eggs Cooked at the Table (page 55), cracking the eggs right onto the hot block before their eyes.

When serving food on a salt block, timing is important so food doesn't sit on the block too long. Food sitting on a warm or room-temperature salt block will absorb salt quickly. To slow the absorption of salt, you can place a buffer, such as a fig leaf or some fresh herbs, between the salt block and the food.

- **TRIVET** A sturdy trivet to rest a hot salt block on is key for serving many recipes. The trivet should be high enough off the table so that the heat from the salt block does not damage the tabletop.

- **LASER THERMOMETER** Personally, I find using a laser thermometer to check the surface temperature of the salt block unnecessary and more of a novelty, but there are those who find this a useful tool.

- **WIRE SCOURING PAD** A basic metal scouring pad will help you remove bits of food stuck after cooking, without damaging the salt block.

- **SALT BLOCK HOLDER** While not an essential item, there are benefits to having a metal form that holds a salt block. It makes it easier to lift and move the salt block in and out of an oven or grill. A metal frame is especially useful for supporting the salt block as it ages and eventfully cracks or breaks into pieces.

CHAPTER TWO

USE AND MAINTENANCE

O nce you heat your salt block for the first time, there's no going back. It is never going to have that beautiful salmon-pink color again. Over time, the color will fade and, eventually, it will become dark brown. That doesn't mean it's not still useful; it just won't be as pretty as when you first bought it. Although it may be sad to lose the original color, this transformation serves as a reminder that a salt block is for more than show. My goal is to ensure that you come to appreciate it as a much-used, well-loved kitchen tool.

While a change of color is part of regular wear and tear, in this chapter let's take a closer look at some need-to-know information about salt block maintenance to ensure that you get the most use possible out of that magical slab.

HEATING

The way you heat your salt block will determine how much use you will get from it over time. The amount of time it takes to heat a salt block depends on its overall mass. The more surface area a salt block has, the longer it takes to heat. Similarly, a thicker salt block will take much longer to heat than a thinner one. It's crucial to heat your salt block slowly over low heat. Do not be surprised if you hear an occasional creak or pop as the salt block heats. Always use your best judgment and lower the heat if it sounds as if it is getting too hot too fast.

HEATING YOUR SALT BLOCK FOR THE FIRST TIME

It is very important to take it extra slow the first time you heat your salt block. That initial pre-heating will reduce stress on the block and allow any residual moisture the necessary time to escape. Salt is hygroscopic, meaning it attracts water, so all salt blocks contain some amount of moisture, but there's no way of knowing exactly how much. I recommend placing your salt block on the burner over low heat for an hour. This will raise the salt block's temperature slowly and release most of its moisture. An extra benefit is you will get a sense of how long it takes for your salt block to heat.

Every time you heat your salt block thereafter, whether to use it on the stovetop, on the grill, or in the oven, it's still important to heat it slowly so that it absorbs the heat evenly. This slow heating reduces the risk of salt block fatigue and breakage and ensures an evenly heated surface.

ON THE STOVETOP

A gas stovetop works best for heating a salt block, but it can be done on an electric range, too. On a gas stove, center the salt block on a burner and place the heat on medium-low. Wait 10 to 15 minutes and then raise the heat to medium, allowing the block to heat for another 10 minutes.

The amount of time it takes to heat your salt block will depend on the size (surface area and thickness) and the type of stove you have. Here are the general times for a 12-by-8-by-1½-inch salt block heated on a gas burner:

- **LOW HEAT** 15 minutes (on a medium flame)

- **MEDIUM HEAT** 20 minutes (15 minutes on a medium flame and 5 minutes on a medium-high flame)

- **MEDIUM-HIGH HEAT** 25 minutes (15 minutes on a medium flame, 5 minutes on a medium-high flame, and 5 minutes on a high flame)

- **HIGH HEAT** 30 minutes (15 minutes on a medium flame, 5 minutes on a medium-high flame, and 10 minutes on a high flame)

If you have an electric range, you will need to raise the salt block so that it is not in direct contact with the heating element. Invert a cast iron pan over the burner or use the outside ring of a springform pan. Place the salt block on the raised surface and gently heat it as you would on a gas burner. Use a laser thermometer or your best judgment to gauge if the block is hot enough to begin cooking. If not, allow the salt block to heat for another 5 minutes and check again.

ON THE GRILL

Both gas and charcoal grills will heat your salt block, but as with the stovetop, a gas grill works better and takes less time because you can easily control the heat and heat the salt block gradually. It's as simple as scraping the grill clean and heating the salt block just as you would over a gas stovetop burner.

A charcoal grill adds more flavor to your food, since it creates smoke, but it is trickier to use. Light the coals on one side of the grill. Once the flame is out, place the salt block on the grill grate on the other side of the grill. As the coals get hotter and the salt block heats, gradually move it closer to the embers. Once the salt block is hot, spread the coals evenly underneath the salt block. Alternatively, to reduce the amount of charcoal needed to grill with a salt block, preheat the salt block on your stovetop (see above for guidelines). Once it is hot, transfer it to the grill grate directly over the hot coals.

IN THE OVEN

Never attempt to heat a salt block directly in an oven. Ovens are naturally humid, especially gas ovens and especially while they are preheating. Salt blocks want to draw in moisture (remember they are hygroscopic), and they can crack or explode if they take on too much moisture too quickly. The safest way to heat your salt block for use in the oven is to first heat it on the stovetop. While the block heats, preheat your oven. Once the salt block and oven are both up to temperature, transfer the salt block to the oven.

HOW TO GAUGE THE TEMPERATURE OF YOUR SALT BLOCK

Unless you have a laser thermometer, I recommend using your personal cooking experience to determine how hot your salt block is. I place my hand over my salt block to get a sense of the temperature much the way I do with a frying pan. With high-temperature cooking, you will want the salt block at around 500°F. If I cannot hold my hand lower than 2 inches from the block surface, then I've reached roughly 500°F. Another good method of testing temperature is by placing a little oil on the block. Canola oil has a smoke point of around 400°F so if it smokes when added you know your block is very hot. It is best to judge the temperature through experience and experimentation, just as you would when cooking with an unfamiliar metal pan. For example, when making pancakes, pour the batter for just one pancake on the block to test how hot it is and adjust the temperature as necessary before making the rest of the pancakes.

MAINTENANCE

Just as with your pots, pans, and favorite kitchen tools, how you maintain your salt block is the best indicator of how long it is likely to last. A salt block needs to be cooled, cleaned, and properly stored to be kept in the best condition for future use.

COOLING

When you have finished cooking with your salt block, turn off the stovetop or grill burner or remove it from the oven. If you move the salt block, place it in a safe, out-of-the-way place on a trivet. A salt block can be slightly warm when you clean it, but given the size and weight of the block, it is easier and safer to wait until it is completely cool. I do not recommend placing the block in the refrigerator or freezer to speed the cooling process. First of all, you risk damaging the interior of the refrigerator. Second, a dense, hot salt block will raise the interior temperature of the refrigerator or freezer, melting or warming other foods that are in close proximity to the heat from the block.

There should be no rush to cool your salt block; it will clean just as easily the next day. It takes about three hours to cool completely, but I often let mine cool overnight before I clean it.

CLEANING

Clean your salt block as you would a well-seasoned cast iron pan. All it needs is a damp metal scouring pad or an abrasive sponge. *Do not use soap and keep the salt block as dry as possible while cleaning.* Moisten the scouring pad with a little water and scrub in small circles to loosen any food stuck to the surface. Wipe the salt block dry with a clean kitchen towel. Take care when cleaning your salt block as water and the scrubbing abrasion will melt and remove some salt from the block. Avoid excessive cleaning and evenly scrub the surface of the block so as to keep it as flat as possible and minimize pitting.

Salt cups and bowls can be cleaned the same way as the block, although cleaning will be much easier. Since cups and bowls are not exposed to heat, bits of food will not be stuck to the surfaces. A quick wipe with a moist sponge will do it. The most important thing is to wipe them completely dry, as any water left sitting in a cup or bowl will dissolve and erode the bottom.

STORAGE

Salt blocks love to absorb water, so you should store yours somewhere that is not humid, well away from moisture. Any good distance away from the sink is fine for most kitchens. You can store it upright or on its side. I often keep one leaning against my cookbooks as an end weight. You can also store your clean, dry salt block in the refrigerator or freezer if you often prepare recipes requiring a chilled salt block. Most refrigerators and freezers are very low in humidity because cold air holds less moisture. However, if you keep a lot of vegetables and leafy greens in your refrigerator, the humidity could be a problem.

WHEN IS IT TIME TO BUY A NEW SALT BLOCK?

With regular use, your salt block will lose its rosy hue. It will have small cracks from repeated heated and cooling. The edges will be chipped from contact with metal surfaces. There will likely be a subtle crater in the center from regular scrubbing—on both sides.

Once your salt block has cracked into too many pieces to be useful or has become too uneven and pitted from regular cleaning, you will want a new block. By the time this happens, you should have a good idea of what kind of cooking you do with your salt block and what type of block is best suited for your purposes. This is a great opportunity to get a thicker salt block or a specific size that suits the way you use it most.

That's not to say there aren't uses for a worn-out salt block. Here are a few that I find helpful:

- Broken pieces work great as weights for pressing foods during cooking.

- Finely grate salt from a block over food; it's salt, after all, and will still season your food.

- Season cooking water with small fragments of the salt block; they will dissolve in hot and boiling water.

- Place a chunk outside as a salt lick for animals.

- Break apart the salt block with a hammer and use it as the salt bed for Beets Roasted on Aromatic Salt (page 75).

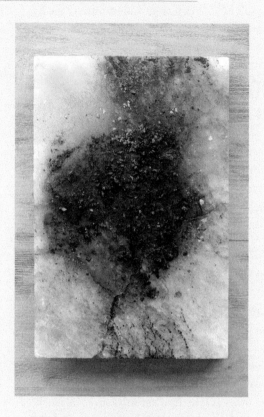

- Grind the salt to use for Whole Fish Roasted in a Salt Crust (page 82).

- Throw a few small pieces in a hot bath and take a relaxing soak.

If your kitchen is especially humid, store the salt block in a resealable plastic bag or wrap it tightly with plastic wrap. You can also store the salt block in a less humid room and use it as decoration.

COMMON SALT BLOCK PITFALLS

Since we've just gone through quite a lot of information about salt block use and care, let's recap the biggest takeaways. Follow these five rules to get the most out of your salt block:

NEVER HEAT THE BLOCK IN THE OVEN This is probably the biggest mistake you can make. During the preheating process, ovens are at their most humid and your salt block will draw in moisture, which will condense on the cool block. As the air around the salt block heats, the cool block will shed water, cooling it more. This stress can cause the salt block to break and even explode. Instead, heat the block on the stovetop and transfer it to the oven only when the block and the oven are at about the same temperature.

MAKE SURE TO FULLY HEAT THE BLOCK If your salt block is too cold when you cook with it, two things will happen. First, the cooler the salt block, the more salt your food will absorb, possibly resulting in overseasoning. Second, meats will not sear or brown and vegetables won't take on enough color. Not only will the foods be less aesthetically pleasing, but they will also be less flavorful.

DRY OFF YOUR INGREDIENTS BEFORE COOKING THEM ON THE BLOCK If ingredients are too wet when they are cooked on a salt block, the residual moisture will draw an excessive amount of salt from the block into your food. While you want your food to take on some salt from the block, you don't want it to absorb too much. Always pat your ingredients dry prior to cooking them.

DON'T LET FOOD SPEND TOO LONG ON THE BLOCK The longer food sits on a salt block, the saltier it becomes. That's great if you're curing foods, but most foods will not benefit from excess contact with the salt. Avoid this problem by eating foods served on a salt block immediately, and by periodically mixing the ingredients to redistribute the salt from the bottom to the top of the food.

AVOID THE "DISAPPEARING SALT BLOCK" TRICK If you use too much water to clean your salt block or put a lot of wet ingredients on your salt block, it will dissolve more quickly and the surface will become uneven. When cleaning your salt block, limit the use of water and avoid aggressive scrubbing. Try to avoid the normal tendency to focus on scrubbing the center of the salt block, or else the surface will become pitted. In addition, it's a good idea to limit the amount of time wet foods are in contact with your salt block, and rotate where on the block you put wet foods. For example, if you serve a lot of dips on your salt block, don't place them right in the center every time.

ABOUT THE RECIPES

Now that you're armed with the necessary salt block cooking tips and tools, it's time to incorporate them into your cooking with approachable recipes you'll want to make. You'll find plenty of recipes to sear, roast, bake, grill, cure, and serve foods with your salt block. Additionally, I've included a few recipes for salt bowls, which are great for salads and dips, and an entire chapter designed specifically for salt cups. Each chapter begins with a techniques overview, along with some quick tips to guide you as you cook.

If you're cooking with a salt block for the first time, I recommend that you pick an easy recipe for your first meal and prepare it twice. You'll learn a lot from the first attempt, and the second time will be even better. Remember that cooking times always vary, as do temperatures of ovens, grills, and the salt blocks themselves. Stick to the basic tips specific to each chapter and your salt block will join the ranks of your favored kitchen tools.

PART TWO **THE RECIPES**

CHAPTER THREE

APPETIZERS AND SIDES

These appetizers and sides are simple but delicious dishes that require only limited preparation and assembly. Since most do not require heating, they are a great way to get to know your salt block.

The natural beauty of salt blocks makes them a unique way to serve food. Just as food looks more appetizing presented on a beautiful plate, your culinary creations will be all the more striking when served on a rosy salt block.

Preparing and serving foods directly on a salt plate is the easiest method of using your salt block. Many of these appetizers and sides are served at room temperature, but I highly recommend chilling your salt block in the refrigerator the day before if you plan on making any chilled appetizers like Tuna Poke with Avocado and Sesame (page 42) or Beef Carpaccio with Parmigiano-Reggiano and Lemon (page 43).

You will learn a lot after preparing a few dishes on your salt block, and you can incorporate what you learn into your regular recipes whenever possible. Don't try to prepare everything on a salt block, but don't be afraid to experiment with how you serve food.

SERVING AND PRESENTATION TIPS

➡ Designate one or two salt blocks just for serving foods. This way their color will not fade from heating and subsequent cooling.

➡ Allow enough time for your salt block to adequately chill. A well-chilled salt block keeps the foods fresher for longer than one hour at room temperature.

➡ Place a chilled salt block on a trivet or folded kitchen towel. The block will likely sweat and may damage surfaces.

➡ Cut ingredients small or thin enough so that they can absorb some salt, but not so small that they become overly salty. Smaller pieces have more surface area that comes in contact with the salt block. In addition, time equals additional seasoning: The longer food is in contact with the salt block, the saltier it becomes. Periodically remix foods like dips to redistribute the salt throughout the food.

➡ Pat ingredients dry when appropriate and don't let them sit on the salt block for extended periods of time. Moisture draws out salt faster at room temperature.

SIMPLE WILTED GREENS

Any fresh greens you have on hand will work for this recipe, but a hearty green like Lacinato kale, Swiss chard, or Bloomsdale spinach will give the best results. The salt block will both cook and season the greens, so seasoning them with additional salt should not be necessary.

SERVES 4

PREP TIME: 5 MINUTES,
PLUS 25 MINUTES TO HEAT
THE SALT BLOCK

COOK TIME: 5 MINUTES

1 bunch leafy greens (about
8 ounces), stems removed

1 tablespoon extra-virgin
olive oil

Chili flakes

1. Gently heat your salt block on the stovetop to medium-high heat, about 25 minutes.

2. In a large bowl, toss the greens with the olive oil and chili flakes. Add a splash of water if the greens are dry (see Tip).

3. Place the greens on the hot salt block. There should be a good burst of steam, which will help wilt the greens. Occasionally turn the greens with a pair of tongs until tender, about 5 minutes, and serve immediately.

TIP The key to wilting is the steam created from the greens when they hit the hot salt block. After washing the greens, let them sit in a colander to drip-dry. Avoid aggressively drying them because some dampness is necessary to generate steam.

TOMATO SALAD
WITH BURRATA

Without salt, tomatoes are acidic and one-dimensional. Once a little salt is added, tomatoes' natural sweetness comes through and the flavors intensify. By serving this salad on a salt block, the tomatoes draw their seasoning from the block and brighten in flavor. Make sure to place a kitchen towel under the block because the tomatoes will release liquid as they take on the salt.

SERVES 4

PREP TIME: 20 MINUTES

1 tablespoon minced shallot

1 tablespoon red wine vinegar

3 large ripe tomatoes

½ pint Sun Gold cherry tomatoes

1 (8-ounce) ball Burrata, at room temperature

Extra-virgin olive oil, for garnish

10 basil leaves, torn, for garnish

Freshly ground black pepper, for garnish

1. Combine the shallot and red wine vinegar in a small bowl and set aside to macerate for 15 minutes.

2. While the shallot is macerating, cut the large tomatoes into ¼-inch-thick slices. Fan them out over a room-temperature salt block.

3. Halve the cherry tomatoes. Flip the tomato slices on the salt block and scatter the cherry tomato halves on and around the sliced tomatoes.

4. Drain the macerated shallot and spoon it over the tomatoes. Break open the Burrata and place it on the salt block.

5. Garnish the tomatoes and Burrata with a drizzle of olive oil. Scatter the basil over everything and season with black pepper. Serve immediately, family-style.

TIP Ripe tomatoes are key to this dish, so it's best prepared when summer is in full swing and tomatoes are at their peak. If you're unable to find Burrata, you can use fresh mozzarella cheese in its place.

FETA SALAD
WITH ZUCCHINI, TOMATO, AND FRESH CORIANDER SEED

At the height of summer, vegetables don't need much more than a little salt in order to make them shine. French feta cheese is a great accompaniment for summer zucchini as it tends to be a little less salty than Greek feta.

SERVES 4

PREP TIME: 20 MINUTES

2 small zucchini, shaved into thin ribbons with a mandoline or vegetable peeler

1 tablespoon fresh green coriander seed (see Tip)

1 garlic clove

8 ounces French feta cheese, cut into ½-inch cubes

1 pint Sun Gold cherry tomatoes, halved

2 tablespoons extra-virgin olive oil

Juice of ½ lemon

Freshly ground black pepper

1. Arrange the shaved zucchini in a single layer on a room-temperature salt block to season, about 3 minutes per side. They should give off a little liquid.

2. While the zucchini seasons on the salt block, combine the coriander and garlic in a mortar and use the pestle to pound them into a coarse paste.

3. Combine the coriander-garlic paste, zucchini, feta, and tomatoes in a large bowl and toss everything with the olive oil and lemon juice. Arrange the salad on the salt block. Season with black pepper and serve.

TIP If you can't find fresh coriander seed, you can substitute 1 teaspoon ground coriander. Toast the coriander before mortaring.

BUCKWHEAT BLINIS
WITH GRAVLAX

Blinis are pancakes with a little yeast added for extra leavening and flavor. They are small, about 1½ inches in diameter, and typically served with caviar or smoked salmon. The addition of the buckwheat flour makes these blinis extra savory, and they cook especially well on a hot salt block. This recipe uses Dill-Cured Salmon Gravlax (page 123), so plan accordingly, or purchase your favorite smoked salmon. These blinis are best enjoyed as an appetizer or as part of a relaxing weekend brunch.

SERVES 4

PREP TIME: 15 MINUTES,
PLUS 1 HOUR TO RISE

COOK TIME: 5 MINUTES

1 cup all-purpose flour

⅓ cup buckwheat flour

2 teaspoons sugar

1 teaspoon active dry yeast

½ teaspoon sea salt

1 cup warm milk (100°F)

3 tablespoons unsalted butter, melted

1 egg, lightly beaten

Canola oil, for coating the block

1 recipe Dill-Cured Salmon Gravlax (page 123), very thinly sliced

Crème fraîche, for garnish

1. Combine the all-purpose flour, buckwheat flour, sugar, yeast, and salt in a large bowl. Add the warm milk and melted butter and mix just until smooth. Avoid overmixing.

2. Cover the bowl with plastic wrap and allow it to sit for 1 hour in a warm, out-of-the-way spot in order to rise, checking after 30 minutes to ensure that it is rising. While the batter is rising for the last 30 minutes, slowly heat your salt block on the stovetop over low heat.

3. Uncover the bowl and add the beaten egg, mixing until it is evenly incorporated.

4. Brush the hot salt block with canola oil and spoon about a tablespoon of batter onto different parts of the block surface. Don't let the blinis run into each other. After about 1 minute, you will see small bubbles forming in the blinis; flip them and cook the other side for about 1 minute more. Remove the blinis to a warm plate and continue to cook the remaining batter in batches.

5. Serve one slice of gravlax, folded in half, on each blini, topped with a dollop of the crème fraîche.

TIP Anything salty or sweet goes well with these blinis, so consider trying other foods like caviar, salmon roe, fruit jams, or ricotta.

GARLICKY ROASTED POTATOES

This dish is simple to make and uses staple ingredients likely already in your kitchen. If your potatoes are larger or you want to reduce the baking time, you can cut them into 1-inch cubes. Just be aware that they will be more likely to stick to the salt block. These potatoes are great served alongside Seared Rib Eye with Salt Block Green Peppercorn Sauce (page 71) or Slow-Roasted Salmon with Whole-Grain Mustard (page 83).

SERVES 4

PREP TIME: 10 MINUTES, PLUS 25 MINUTES TO HEAT THE SALT BLOCK

COOK TIME: 45 MINUTES

1½ pounds new potatoes, such as butterball or fingerling, scrubbed and halved

4 or 5 garlic cloves, smashed

3 or 4 thyme or rosemary sprigs

Sea salt

Freshly ground black pepper

Extra-virgin olive oil

1. Preheat the oven to 400°F. Heat your salt block on the stovetop to medium-high heat, about 25 minutes.

2. Toss the potatoes with the garlic and thyme, and season with salt and black pepper in a large bowl with just enough olive oil to coat the ingredients.

3. Place the hot salt block on a baking sheet (to catch any spills) and arrange the potatoes and seasonings on top of the salt block in an even layer. Place the baking sheet with the salt block on the center rack in the oven and bake until the potatoes are fully cooked and tender, about 45 minutes.

4. Serve immediately or keep warm until ready to serve.

SPICED ALMONDS

Warm almonds make a great party snack and take only a few minutes to prepare, allowing you to be with your guests rather than spending a lot of time in the kitchen. The warmth of the salt block will carry the enticing aromas of the spices throughout your house, and using an extra-thick salt block makes for a dramatic presentation.

MAKES 2 CUPS

PREP TIME: 5 MINUTES,
PLUS 15 MINUTES TO HEAT
THE SALT BLOCK

COOK TIME: 10 MINUTES

2 cups raw almonds

Leaves from 1 rosemary sprig

Extra-virgin olive oil

1 tablespoon smoked pimentón

Coarse sea salt

1. Preheat the oven to 350°F. Heat a salt block on the stovetop to low heat, about 15 minutes.

2. Spread the almonds on a baking sheet and sprinkle them with the rosemary. Bake the almonds until the skins begin to darken and the almonds begin to release their aroma, about 10 minutes.

3. While the almonds are still hot, drizzle them with enough olive oil to coat, and then sprinkle them with the pimentón and sea salt. Give the spiced almonds a quick toss and transfer them to the warm salt block. Serve.

TIP Almonds burn very quickly, so make sure that your serving salt block is only slightly warm, not hot. It should be just warm enough to help activate the aroma of the almonds and spices but not to continue to cook them.

SMASHED POTATO SKINS
WITH CHEDDAR AND SCALLIONS

The key to this dish is using two salt blocks, with the top one acting as a weight to flatten the halved potatoes and season them during baking. That way, both sides of the potatoes absorb salt and get crisp. Then the top salt block is removed so that the cheese can melt.

SERVES 4

PREP TIME: 10 MINUTES,
PLUS 20 MINUTES TO HEAT
THE SALT BLOCK

COOK TIME: 40 MINUTES

4 russet potatoes, each about 3 inches long, scrubbed and halved lengthwise

Canola oil

1 cup shredded Cheddar cheese

½ cup sour cream, for garnish

2 scallions, cut into thin rings, for garnish

1. Preheat the oven to 375°F. Gently heat two salt blocks on the stovetop to medium heat, about 20 minutes.

2. Meanwhile, put the potatoes in a saucepan and cover with cold water. Set the pan over medium-high heat and bring the water to a boil. Reduce the heat to a simmer and cook the potatoes until very tender, 15 to 20 minutes. Remove the potatoes and set them aside until cool enough to handle, then scoop out the flesh (reserve it for another use, like mashed potatoes).

3. Place one of the hot salt blocks on a rimmed baking sheet. Lightly oil the potato skins on both sides and place them cut-side down on the salt block. Place the second hot salt block on top of the potatoes. Transfer the baking sheet with the salt block sandwich to the oven and bake for 20 minutes.

4. Remove the top salt block and flip the potato skins so the cut sides are facing up. Sprinkle each with the Cheddar cheese and return the bottom salt block with the potato skins to the oven for 3 minutes, until the cheese has melted. Serve immediately with the sour cream and scallions for garnish.

TIP For a more filling snack, use whole potatoes rather than just the skins: Lightly smash each boiled potato half with the back of a fork or the palm of your hand so that they are roughly ½ inch thick, taking care that they do not fall apart. Then continue with steps 3 and 4 of the recipe.

SALTED LIME GUACAMOLE
WITH TORTILLA CHIPS

Mixing the guacamole on the salt block pulls more flavor out of the lime zest and mellows the raw garlic. As the guacamole sits on the salt block, scoop it from the bottom of the block onto your tortilla chip, redistributing the salt to the mixture not resting on the block. This will keep the whole dish evenly seasoned.

SERVES 4

PREP TIME: 15 MINUTES,
PLUS 10 MINUTES TO REST

Grated zest and juice
of 2 limes, divided

1 large garlic clove, minced

2 large avocados

½ medium yellow onion, diced

2 Roma tomatoes, diced

½ jalapeño, seeded and minced

1 tablespoon chopped
fresh cilantro

1 teaspoon cayenne pepper

Sea salt

Tortilla chips, for serving

1. Combine the zest from both limes, 1 teaspoon of lime juice, and the garlic on a room-temperature salt block. Using the back of a fork, mash them together. Let the mixture rest for 10 minutes.

2. Halve and pit the avocados and scoop the flesh onto the salt block with the garlic mixture. Add the onion, tomatoes, jalapeño, cilantro, and cayenne pepper and mix and mash everything until well incorporated. Season the guacamole with sea salt and some of the remaining lime juice. Serve immediately with tortilla chips.

TIP The guacamole does not spend enough time on the salt block to be fully seasoned, so don't be stingy with the sea salt. The salt and lime juice are keys to balancing out the avocado's richness so don't be afraid to add more of either.

BITTER CITRUS CONDIMENT

This recipe makes a deliciously savory condiment that can be served in place of salsa or relish. I like to serve it alongside poultry or lamb, or richer white fish like cod or sea bass. It also goes great on a slice of hearty toast in place of jam. Cooking the citrus on a salt block seasons and blackens the citrus, making it both sweet and sour. Store in a tightly sealed container in the refrigerator for up to a month.

MAKES ABOUT 1 CUP

PREP TIME: 10 MINUTES, PLUS 25 MINUTES TO HEAT THE SALT BLOCK

COOK TIME: 10 MINUTES

Canola oil, for coating the block

2 lemons, washed and cut crosswise into ¼-inch-thick slices

2 oranges, washed and cut crosswise into ¼-inch-thick slices

2 tablespoons champagne vinegar

2 tablespoons extra-virgin olive oil

Sea salt

1. Slowly heat your salt block on the stovetop to medium-high heat, about 25 minutes. Once it is hot, brush it with the canola oil, arrange the citrus slices in a single layer on the salt block, and increase the temperature to high.

2. Allow the citrus to take on as much color as possible before turning the slices, about 5 minutes per side. The rind should be tender. Slight burning adds bitterness, which is a nice counterpoint to the sweetness.

3. Once fully cooked on both sides, transfer the citrus to a cutting board. While still hot, roughly chop the citrus. Drizzle with the vinegar and olive oil and mix everything to form a chunky paste. Season with salt if necessary.

TIP Experiment with different types of citrus and ratios. For example, grapefruit is a great way to increase bitterness—try an equal amount of grapefruit, orange, and lemon slices.

SIMPLE FISH CRUDO

This is a great first recipe to try on your salt block, especially if you are a little reluctant to eat raw fish. Ask a trusted seafood purveyor for the freshest fish they can recommend for eating raw—center-cut fillet portions are best. Have them remove any skin or bones. I usually slice the fish similar to Japanese nigiri, but it can also be diced and eaten like tartare, with toast or crackers.

SERVES 4

PREP TIME: 15 MINUTES,
PLUS OVERNIGHT TO CHILL
THE SALT BLOCK

Juice of 1 lemon

3 tablespoons finely diced shallot

1 (1-pound) very fresh fish fillet

Coarse sea salt

Freshly ground black pepper

Extra-virgin olive oil

1. Chill a salt block in the freezer, preferably overnight.

2. Combine the lemon juice and shallot in a small bowl. Let the shallot marinate for 10 minutes.

3. Meanwhile, cut the fish lengthwise into 1½- to 2-inch sections. Then cut these sections into slices no thicker than ¼ inch. Fan out the slices across the cold salt block. Season the fish with salt and black pepper.

4. Drain the shallot and spoon it over the fish. Generously drizzle everything with the olive oil. Serve immediately.

TIP Personalize the service by using four small salt blocks—give each person their own serving. Pieces of a broken salt block work well for individual servings.

TUNA POKE
WITH AVOCADO AND SESAME

Poke is a Hawaiian fish salad that is served raw, often as an appetizer or an hors d'oeuvre. Although it is usually made with yellowfin tuna, the key to success is using the freshest fish available. Here, the salt block aids in seasoning the fish and marinating it with the other ingredients.

SERVES 4

PREP TIME: 15 MINUTES,
PLUS OVERNIGHT TO CHILL
THE SALT BLOCK

1 tablespoon black sesame seeds, plus more for garnish

1 tablespoon white sesame seeds, plus more for garnish

2 tablespoons coarsely ground candlenuts, plus more for garnish (see Tip)

1 pound sushi-grade yellowfin tuna, cut into ½-inch cubes

1 avocado, peeled, pitted, and cut into ¼-inch cubes

⅓ cup finely diced sweet onion, such as Maui or Walla Walla

5 teaspoons toasted sesame oil

3 teaspoons low-sodium soy sauce

Dried seaweed, for garnish

Rice crackers, for serving (optional)

1. Chill a salt block in the freezer, preferably overnight.

2. Toast the black and white sesame seeds, and candlenuts on a hot salt block or in a cast iron pan until they are fragrant and just beginning to brown. Reserve 1 tablespoon for a garnish.

3. Transfer the sesame seed mixture to a large bowl. Add the tuna, avocado, onion, sesame oil, and soy sauce to the bowl and mix everything together.

4. Transfer the poke to the cold salt block and garnish it with the dried seaweed and reserved 1 tablespoon of sesame seed mixture. Serve the poke family style; it can be eaten with a fork or with rice crackers.

TIP Candlenuts, or candleberries, are a common ingredient in Hawaiian, Indonesian, and Malaysian cooking. Look for them in health food stores or Asian markets. If you cannot find candlenuts, substitute macadamia nuts. Both are oily nuts, which add texture and richness to this dish.

BEEF CARPACCIO
WITH PARMIGIANO-REGGIANO AND LEMON

If you enjoy a medium-rare steak, there's no reason you won't love this beef carpaccio. Use a tender cut of beef such as tenderloin or eye of round. It's best to slice the beef just before serving, but don't be afraid to ask your butcher for assistance in selecting or cutting the beef.

SERVES 4

PREP TIME: 10 MINUTES,
PLUS 10 MINUTES TO CHILL
THE SALT BLOCK

10 ounces lean tender beef, sliced as thinly as possible against the grain (see Tip)

1 bunch arugula

1 (3-ounce) block Parmigiano-Reggiano

Coarse sea salt, for garnish

Freshly ground black pepper, for garnish

1 lemon, for garnish

Extra-virgin olive oil, for garnish

1 baguette, sliced, oiled, and toasted

1. Chill your salt block in the freezer for 10 minutes.

2. Arrange the beef slices in a single layer on the chilled salt block. Layer the arugula over the beef. Use a vegetable peeler to shave the Parmesan over the arugula.

3. Season the carpaccio with salt, black pepper, a squeeze of lemon, and a generous drizzle of olive oil. Serve immediately with the toasted baguette slices.

TIP The easiest way to thinly slice beef is to first freeze it for 10 minutes. It firms the beef, making it easier to cut. Be sure to use a very sharp knife and make long, even cuts against the grain.

BUTTERMILK DRESSING

Make your everyday salad more interesting with this zippy dressing. It's creamy and delicious without being heavy. It goes best with mild crisp greens like butter lettuce or Little Gem lettuce—really, anything crunchy enough that you can coat the leaves with dressing and not have it all go soggy. Make the dressing in a salt bowl and serve it next to the salad so everyone can get just the right amount of dressing.

MAKES ABOUT 2 CUPS

PREP TIME: 15 MINUTES,
PLUS 10 MINUTES TO CHILL
THE SALT BOWL

4 garlic cloves, mortared
to a paste

1 cup buttermilk

1 cup nonfat yogurt or
sour cream

Lots of freshly ground
black pepper

1. Chill a salt bowl in the freezer for 10 minutes.

2. Put the garlic in the chilled salt bowl and stir it slightly to salt it. Let it rest for 5 minutes.

3. Whisk in the buttermilk and yogurt and add a generous amount of black pepper. Let it sit for 5 minutes.

4. Adjust the seasoning and serve immediately.

TIP Letting the dressing sit gives it enough time to draw out the salt from the bowl before you dress the salad. The dressing is very acidic and needs a healthy amount of salt to be balanced.

CELERY ROOT REMOULADE

Think of this simple dish as coleslaw that uses celery root (also known as celeriac) instead of cabbage. The salt from the bowl helps season and soften the celery root. Just mix the raw ingredients in the bowl and let the salt and time do the rest of the work. This dish is best served alongside a light entrée such as poultry, pork, or fish. If you prefer a richer, more traditional remoulade, add ½ cup mayonnaise in step 2.

SERVES 4

PREP TIME: 15 MINUTES, PLUS 10 TO 20 MINUTES TO MARINATE

1 large celery root bulb, peeled

¼ cup extra-virgin olive oil

2 tablespoons freshly squeezed lemon juice or champagne vinegar

2 tablespoons whole-grain mustard

1 tablespoon capers, drained and chopped

1 tablespoon chopped fresh parsley

1 tablespoon celery seeds (optional)

1. Using a food processor or box grater, grate the celery root using the largest setting. Transfer the celery root to a large room-temperature salt bowl.

2. Add the olive oil, lemon juice, mustard, capers, parsley, and celery seeds (if using) to the salt bowl. Stir everything to mix well.

3. Cover the salt bowl with a clean kitchen towel or plastic wrap and let it sit at room temperature until it reaches your desired texture, 10 to 20 minutes (see Tip). Serve in the salt bowl.

TIP The longer the remoulade sits in the bowl, the saltier and softer it becomes so stir and taste it often. Consider transferring the remoulade to a glass bowl for a portion of the marinating time if you like the celery root on the softer side but have already achieved your desired saltiness—it will continue to soften on its own.

SEA BASS CEVICHE
WITH RED ONION AND CORN

Ceviche is a seafood dish where the raw fish is "cooked" from the acid in citrus juice. This dish has its roots in Peru but is very popular all over Latin America. During my travels in Peru, I ate ceviche nearly every day for two weeks without growing tired of its simple flavors. Regardless of where it was served, it always contained sea bass, lemon, red onion, and corn. This is a great dish to tempt less adventurous eaters who may be wary of eating raw fish.

SERVES 4

PREP TIME: 10 MINUTES,
PLUS 10 MINUTES TO CHILL
THE SALT BOWL

1 pound white sea bass, cut into ½-inch cubes

½ cup fresh corn kernels

½ jalapeño, seeded and very thinly sliced

½ red onion, very thinly sliced

½ cup freshly squeezed lemon or lime juice

24 to 36 fresh cilantro leaves, divided

1. Chill a salt bowl in the freezer for 10 minutes while you prepare the ingredients.

2. Combine the sea bass, corn, jalapeño, onion, and lemon juice in the chilled salt bowl. Refrigerate the ceviche for 5 minutes.

3. Remix the ceviche with half the cilantro. Garnish with the remaining cilantro. Serve immediately.

TIP If you do not have a salt bowl, you can use a chilled salt block. Make the ceviche in a glass bowl and add 2 teaspoons coarse sea salt with the ingredients in step 2. Use a slotted spoon to transfer the ceviche to the chilled salt block, leaving behind the excess liquid.

CHICKEN CAESAR SALAD

Homemade Caesar salad dressing is sublime. Once you've had it, you'll never go back to the bottled stuff. The base of this dressing is *aioli*, which is very easy to make, and once you master preparing it, you'll find dozens of ways to use it.

SERVES 4

PREP TIME: 10 MINUTES, PLUS 2 HOURS TO CHILL THE SALT BOWL

1 garlic clove

7 salt-packed anchovy fillets, such as Agostino Recca, rinsed

2 egg yolks

1 cup mild extra-virgin olive oil

Juice of 1 lemon

Sea salt

Freshly ground black pepper

2 cooked chicken breasts, cut into 1-inch cubes

3 romaine lettuce hearts, coarsely chopped

1 cup grated Parmesan cheese

Freshly toasted croutons

1. Chill a large salt bowl or salt block in the refrigerator for at least 2 hours.

2. To make the dressing, combine the garlic and anchovy fillets in a mortar and use the pestle to mash them together into a paste. Set aside.

3. Put the egg yolks in a medium bowl. Very slowly drip in the olive oil while continually whisking it with the egg yolks. This allows the yolks to absorb the oil, ensuring you have a creamy dressing. When the dressing begins to get stiff and a little dull in color (this may happen before all the olive oil has been added), whisk in the lemon juice and then finish whisking in any remaining oil. Add the garlic-anchovy paste and whisk until it is evenly incorporated. Season the dressing with salt and black pepper.

4. Combine the chicken cubes, romaine, Parmesan cheese, and croutons in the chilled salt bowl. Drizzle the dressing over the salad and toss until everything is coated. Adjust the seasoning if needed, and serve.

TIP Adding the olive oil very slowly at the beginning will prevent the *aioli* from breaking.

CHILLED GAZPACHO
SERVED IN SALT CUPS

Offer this no-cook soup as an hors d'oeuvre to guests the next time you grill in the backyard. Tomatoes love, and need, to be well salted in order to balance their acidity, so serving this gazpacho in salt cups only improves the flavor.

SERVES 8

PREP TIME: 20 MINUTES, PLUS OVERNIGHT TO CHILL THE SOUP AND SALT CUPS

1 small garlic clove

8 basil leaves

2 tablespoons red wine vinegar, divided, plus additional if needed

4 to 6 large, very ripe tomatoes

¼ cup extra-virgin olive oil, plus 2 tablespoons

1 tablespoon finely diced shallot, for garnish

1 tablespoon finely diced cucumber, for garnish

1 tablespoon finely diced red or green bell pepper, for garnish

Sea salt

1. Combine the garlic and basil in a mortar and use the pestle to mash them together to form a paste. Add 1 tablespoon of the red wine vinegar to the mortar and stir it into the garlic-basil paste. Set aside.

2. Halve the tomatoes crosswise. Using the largest setting of a box grater, shred the tomatoes into a large bowl. Place a strainer fine enough to collect the tomato seeds over another large bowl. Pass the tomatoes through the strainer and discard the seeds.

3. Add the garlic mixture to the strainer and press it hard to extract as much liquid as possible. Add ¼ cup of olive oil to the bowl and stir to combine. Cover and refrigerate overnight. Put eight salt cups in the refrigerator to chill at the same time.

4. The next day, make the garnish. Combine the diced shallot and the remaining 1 tablespoon of red wine vinegar in a small bowl and set aside to macerate for at least 15 minutes. Drain the shallot and return it to the bowl. Add the cucumber, bell pepper, and remaining 2 tablespoons of olive oil and stir to combine. Set the garnish aside.

5. Taste the cold soup and adjust the seasoning with sea salt and more vinegar, if needed (see Tip). Remember that the soup will take on salt from the cup when served, so leaving it a little undersalted is recommended.

6. Pour the gazpacho into the chilled salt cups and garnish each serving with a bit of the vegetable garnish. Serve immediately.

TIP The key to seasoning the gazpacho is to taste it the way it will be served: Pour a little soup into a cold salt cup and taste, then adjust the seasoning accordingly.

STOVETOP COOKING

Using your salt block on the stovetop is the easiest heating technique you'll learn in this book, and likely the most frequent way you put your salt block to use. A heated salt block provides very even heat, allowing you to brown the outsides of meats and vegetables as well as, if not better than, any pan.

It's imperative to take time to properly heat the salt block before use, so the first step in all the recipes to follow will be to slowly heat the block to the heat level needed to successfully prepare the dish. By the time you are finished prepping the ingredients, the salt block will be ready for cooking.

Salt blocks heat best over gas burners. Start with the burner on medium-low heat and gradually increase the temperature every five minutes or so until the block has reached your desired temperature. See page 20 for general guidelines on how long it takes to heat your salt block to different temperatures before you get started.

If you have an electric or flat glass-top stove, raise the block about an inch from the heating element—using the outer ring of a springform pan works very well.

Over time it is normal for the surface of your salt block to become slightly pitted. Although you want to avoid distorting the surface too much, creating a slight valley in the block is helpful for trapping oil or any sauces you create on the salt block rather than having it run off the sides. Keep this in mind when cleaning your salt block—intentionally create a dip in the center of one salt block and use this block for cooking foods that are prone to release liquid during cooking.

STOVETOP COOKING TIPS

➡ Over time you will learn to gauge the surface temperature of your block and you'll know how long it takes to heat to the needed temperature. Until you get to this point of familiarity, always test the temperature before cooking on the block. If the block is not hot enough, your food will not cook properly and will absorb more salt.

➡ Foods can stick to a salt block just as they can to a pan. The trick is to lightly oil the block once it is hot and to pat foods dry before placing them on the salt block. Once browned, the food should easily turn. If it sticks to the salt block, then it is not ready to turn. Give it a little more time to cook and it will release from the block as the outside dries and a crust is formed.

➡ Sometime foods need a little extra salt. Just as when you cook in a pan, taste the finished dish and adjust the seasoning if necessary. Unlike a room-temperature or chilled salt block, a heated salt block will not oversalt the food cooked on it. Often slices of roasted meat will want a little extra salt. Fan them over the salt block and grate a broken piece of salt block over them for a finishing touch.

➡ Salt is not a great heat conductor, so once heated it is slow to release that heat. After you've used your salt block to sear a piece of meat, take advantage of the residual heat to cook something else.

ASPARAGUS
WITH SHAVED PARMIGIANO-REGGIANO AND BALSAMIC

Asparagus is probably my favorite vegetable to cook on a salt block. As it roasts, the outside of the asparagus becomes nutty and the inside becomes delightfully tender. Although you can buy asparagus year round, I advise against it. It's worth waiting until spring to get local asparagus, which is sweet and tender rather than the bland, off-season, grown-halfway-around-the-world asparagus.

SERVES 4

PREP TIME: 10 MINUTES, PLUS 30 MINUTES TO HEAT THE SALT BLOCK

COOK TIME: 5 TO 10 MINUTES

2 bunches asparagus, bottom third removed

Canola oil

1 (3-ounce) piece Parmigiano-Reggiano

Aged balsamic vinegar, such as Villa Manodori

1. Heat your salt block on the stovetop to high heat, about 30 minutes.

2. In a large bowl, toss the asparagus with just enough canola oil to coat each stalk. Spread the asparagus evenly on the hot salt block. As the asparagus begins to color and the outside begins to lightly brown, turn the stalks to roast them all around.

3. Once lightly browned all around, transfer the asparagus to a large flat serving dish or leave on the hot salt block to serve. Using a vegetable peeler, shave the Parmigiano-Reggiano over the asparagus and drizzle them with the balsamic vinegar. Serve either hot or at room temperature.

TIP The ideal asparagus will be roughly the diameter of your pinky finger and very tender. If your asparagus is larger, or you find it to be tough, blanch the asparagus in salted water for 30 seconds before cooking on the hot salt block.

OLIVE OIL TORTILLAS

The salt block adds a hint of salt to fresh tortillas. These are great served with eggs, or add a little shredded cheese to make a quesadilla. If you have a large rectangular block, you can cook more than one tortilla at a time.

SERVES 4

PREP TIME: 5 MINUTES,
PLUS 20 MINUTES TO HEAT
THE SALT BLOCK

COOK TIME: 30 MINUTES

8 corn tortillas

Extra-virgin olive oil

1. Gently heat your salt block on the stovetop to medium heat, about 20 minutes.

2. Generously oil both sides of a tortilla and place it on the salt block. Keep the flame beneath the salt block on low to allow the tortilla to gently crisp without burning. Once the first side of the tortilla is lightly crisped, 2 to 3 minutes, turn it and crisp the other side, 2 to 3 minutes more. Serve immediately, and repeat for the remaining tortillas.

TIP Even a salt block can't rejuvenate a stale tortilla. This preparation is all about using the very freshest of tortillas.

SUNNY-SIDE UP EGGS
COOKED AT THE TABLE

Ever declared it's hot enough to fry an egg on the sidewalk? Well, you can certainly do it on a hot salt block. The salt block needs to be screaming hot to prepare these eggs, so make sure it's in a safe place on the table and out of the reach of children.

SERVES 4

PREP TIME: 5 MINUTES PER EGG, PLUS 30 MINUTES TO HEAT THE SALT BLOCK

COOK TIME: 8 MINUTES

Canola oil, for coating the block

8 eggs

Sea salt

Freshly ground black pepper

1. Gently heat a salt block on the stovetop to high heat, about 30 minutes. Once it is very hot, carefully move it onto a trivet or folded kitchen towel at the table.

2. Generously brush the salt block with canola oil. The block should smoke right away when the oil is added. Working in batches of 3 or 4 eggs, crack the eggs directly onto the salt block. Cook them until the whites are firm but the yolks are still soft, about 4 minutes. Season with sea salt and black pepper and serve immediately. Generously re-oil the salt block and repeat for the remaining eggs. If the salt block has been sitting for too long between batches, reheat it until it is at high heat again.

TIP A metal bowl can be inverted over the eggs to trap the heat and cook the eggs faster or cook the yolks more for anyone who doesn't like a very runny yolk. An inverted bowl works great for any foods that do not lie completely flat on the salt block surface and thus have less direct contact with the heat.

GRILLED CHEESE
WITH HAM

Grilled cheese with ham was one of my favorite things to eat as a child, and it's still a comfort food. Here, the gentle heat from the salt block toasts the bread evenly and imparts a little extra salty kick. Since you'll spend as much time heating the salt block as prepping and cooking the sandwiches, take advantage of the hot salt block after you've finished making your grilled cheese and bake some Peanut Butter Cookies (page 140) or a Quick Berry Tart (page 147).

SERVES 4

PREP TIME: 5 MINUTES, PLUS 15 MINUTES TO HEAT THE SALT BLOCK

COOK TIME: 6 MINUTES

A hearty loaf of bread, such as levain

Unsalted butter, at room temperature

8 (1-ounce) slices mild Cheddar cheese

4 (1¼-ounces) slices ham

1. Gently heat a salt block on the stovetop to low heat, about 15 minutes.

2. Slice the bread into eight ½-inch-thick slices. Generously butter one side of each bread slice. Place four of the bread slices butter-side down on the hot salt block. Place a slice of cheese on each of the bread slices, followed by a slice of ham and a second slice of the cheese. Top each sandwich with a second bread slice, butter-side up.

3. When the bottom slices of bread begin to brown, about 3 minutes, flip the sandwiches and brown the second side, about 3 minutes more. Serve immediately.

TIP Gently heat a second salt block or a portion of a broken block and place it on top of the sandwiches. The additional heat and pressure will help melt the cheese.

CORNMEAL PANCAKES
WITH HONEY

The salt these pancakes absorb as they cook on the salt block offsets the sweetness of the cornmeal, resulting in the perfect balance of salty and sweet. If you find that the pancakes take on a little too much salt for your taste, serve them with a little extra crème fraîche or whipped cream. This recipe is especially decadent, so it makes a great holiday breakfast.

SERVES 4

PREP TIME: 10 MINUTES,
PLUS 20 MINUTES TO HEAT
THE SALT BLOCK

COOK TIME: 10 MINUTES

1 cup all-purpose flour

½ cup fine stone-ground cornmeal

1¼ teaspoons baking powder

½ teaspoon baking soda

1½ cups buttermilk

1 egg, lightly beaten

4 tablespoons unsalted butter, melted, divided

¼ cup honey, preferably unfiltered, plus additional for garnish

Crème fraîche, for garnish

1. Preheat your salt block on the stovetop to medium heat, about 20 minutes.

2. In a large bowl, combine the flour, cornmeal, baking powder, and baking soda. In a medium bowl, whisk together the buttermilk, egg, 3 tablespoons of melted butter, and the honey. Add the wet ingredients to the dry ingredients. Mix everything together until just combined. Do not overmix; some small clumps of flour are normal.

3. Brush the hot salt block with the remaining 1 tablespoon of melted butter. Spoon about ¼ cup of batter onto the salt block for each pancake. Once small bubbles begin to appear in the center of the pancakes and the bottoms begin to brown, about 1 minute, flip them. Cook the second side of the pancakes until the bottoms begin to brown, about 1 minute more.

4. Transfer the pancakes to a warm serving plate and garnish with more honey and crème fraîche. Serve immediately.

TIP The temperature of the salt block is key for cooking pancakes. I recommend making a tester pancake to ensure the block is at the right temperature. If it's too hot, the sugars in the batter will burn before the pancakes are cooked through; if it's too cool, the pancakes will be flat and pale. If the tester pancake doesn't turn out the way you want it to, adjust the temperature of your salt block as needed.

SCALLION PANCAKES

These savory pancakes are delicious on their own or served alongside poultry cooked on a salt block. I like to have a few as a pre-dinner snack with plum dipping sauce, then save the rest to eat with duck breast cooked on the preheated salt block.

SERVES 4

PREP TIME: 20 MINUTES,
PLUS 65 MINUTES TO REST

COOK TIME: 3 MINUTES

1 ¼ cups all-purpose flour

½ cup warm water

Canola oil, for oiling the dough and coating the block

1 bunch scallions, cut into thin rings

1. In a medium bowl, mix the flour and water together to form a dough. Knead the dough until it is smooth and elastic, about 5 minutes. Lightly oil the outside of the dough, place it in a bowl, and cover the bowl with plastic wrap. Set the bowl aside and let the dough rest for at least 45 minutes.

2. On a clean, flat surface, use a rolling pin to roll out the dough to ⅛-inch thickness. Sprinkle the scallions over the dough and then roll the dough into a log. Set the dough log aside to rest for at least 20 minutes.

3. Meanwhile, preheat your salt block on the stovetop to medium-high heat, about 25 minutes.

4. Cut the dough log into ½-inch-thick rounds. Lightly oil one side of each round and use the rolling pin to roll out each round as thin as possible, about ⅛ inch thick.

5. Brush the hot salt block with canola oil. Place the pancakes on the salt block and cook until the bottom of the pancake has blistered, about 1½ minutes. Flip the pancakes and cook until the second side begins to blister, about 1½ minutes more. Serve.

TIP The longer you rest the dough in between stages the better. The longer it rests, the easier it is to roll it out as thinly as possible. This results in a more tender scallion pancake.

BLACKENED CATFISH

Blackened catfish is all about lots of seasoning and a high-heat sear. A ripping-hot salt block is a great way to give the fish an intense sear. Don't be afraid to generously coat the catfish with the spice mixture. The high heat of the salt block will blacken and intensify the spices.

SERVES 4

PREP TIME: 5 MINUTES, PLUS 30 MINUTES TO HEAT THE SALT BLOCK

COOK TIME: 3 MINUTES

2 teaspoons sweet paprika

2 teaspoons dried thyme

2 teaspoons dried oregano

½ teaspoon cayenne pepper

½ teaspoon freshly ground black pepper

4 catfish fillets

Canola oil

1. Gently heat your salt block on the stovetop to high heat, about 30 minutes.

2. In a small bowl, combine the paprika, thyme, oregano, cayenne pepper, and black pepper. Pat the catfish fillets dry and then coat them on both sides with the spice mixture. Lightly brush the fish with oil if the spices have trouble sticking.

3. Place the coated catfish fillets on the hot salt block and sear them for about 1½ minutes. Flip the fillets and sear the second side for about 1½ minutes. Serve immediately.

TIP This makes a delicious lunch when served on a soft roll with mayonnaise or a satisfying dinner with some "dirty" rice on the side.

TERIYAKI-GLAZED SALMON
WITH BLACK SESAME

Sweet and sour is a great combination with the mildness of salmon. Making your own teriyaki sauce is simple, and I recommend making a larger batch since it keeps well in the refrigerator and tastes great on a variety of meats, too. Given the salty nature of salt block cooking, I suggest using a low-sodium soy sauce.

SERVES 4

PREP TIME: 10 MINUTES, PLUS 20 MINUTES TO HEAT THE SALT BLOCK

COOK TIME: 10 MINUTES

1 cup water

¼ cup low-sodium soy sauce

¼ cup honey, preferably unfiltered

2 tablespoons brown sugar

1 teaspoon garlic powder

1 teaspoon ground ginger

2 tablespoons cornstarch whisked into ¼ cup cold water

4 (6-ounce) salmon fillets, skin and bloodline removed

Canola oil

½ cup black sesame seeds

1. Gently heat the salt block on the stovetop to medium heat, about 20 minutes.

2. To make the teriyaki sauce, heat the water, soy sauce, honey, brown sugar, garlic powder, and ginger in a small saucepan over low heat. Once the honey and sugar have dissolved, bring the sauce to a boil and stir in the cornstarch mixture. Continue to cook the sauce over low heat until it has thickened. If it becomes too thick, adjust the consistency with a little water.

3. Pat the fish fillets dry and lightly oil them on both sides. Roll each fillet in the sesame seeds, making sure to coat both sides completely. You may need to press the sesame seeds gently into the fillets to make sure they stick. Place the fillets on the hot salt block and cook until the fish is just warmed inside, about 5 minutes per side. Glaze the top of each fillet with the warm teriyaki sauce and serve immediately.

TIP Cooking salmon properly is easy if you have a metal cake tester. Slide the cake tester into the center of the fillet and wait 5 seconds. Remove the tester and gently touch it to your lower lip. If it feels warm, the fish is done. If you want the fish cooked all the way through, allow it to cook for an additional minute or two.

DAY BOAT SCALLOPS
WITH WILTED ARUGULA AND LIME

With fresh scallops, there's not much you need to do to make a delicious meal. Day boat scallops are harvested on a small boat that docks at the end of the day rather than staying out overnight. The scallops are pricey, but their freshness and quality are well worth a few extra dollars. The salt block gives the scallops a nice golden brown color and adds flavor to their natural briny taste.

SERVES 4

PREP TIME: 5 MINUTES,
PLUS 30 MINUTES TO HEAT
THE SALT BLOCK

COOK TIME: 5 MINUTES

Canola oil, for coating the block

12 large day boat scallops, abductors removed

2 bunches thick-leafed arugula (about 8 ounces each)

Extra-virgin olive oil

2 limes, quartered

1. Gently heat a salt block on the stovetop to high heat, about 30 minutes.

2. Brush the salt block with canola oil. Use a paper towel to pat the scallops dry and place them on the salt block. Sear them for about 1 minute per side. Each side of the scallop should take on a dark brown crust but stay tender in the center. Remove the scallops and set aside.

3. In a large bowl, toss the arugula with some olive oil and place it on the salt block. Repeatedly turn the arugula to wilt it. The total time should be less than a minute.

4. Divide the arugula among four plates and place 3 scallops each on top of the arugula. Squeeze a lime quarter over the scallops and garnish each plate with an additional lime quarter. Serve immediately.

TIP A very hot salt block and very dry scallops are key to ensuring that the scallops sear without sticking. Additionally, do not oil the salt block until it is very hot. This helps create a nonstick surface.

SALT AND PEPPER SHRIMP

This is a new take on cocktail shrimp. Present this at a party and your guests will be huddled around the serving dish. Serve with your favorite cocktail sauce or break out all the stops and make your own.

SERVES 4

PREP TIME: 5 MINUTES,
PLUS 30 MINUTES TO HEAT
THE SALT BLOCK

COOK TIME: 1 MINUTE

1 pound large shrimp
(31 to 35), shell-on

Canola oil

Freshly ground black pepper

1 lemon, cut into wedges,
for garnish

Cocktail sauce, for garnish

1. Gently heat a salt block on the stovetop to high heat, about 30 minutes.

2. In a large bowl, toss the shrimp with just enough oil to coat. Spread the shrimp over the hot salt block. Cook them for about 30 seconds per side. Do not overcook the shrimp. They will cook faster than you expect and will continue to cook after they are removed from the salt block.

3. Transfer the shrimp to a serving bowl and generously season them with black pepper. Serve with the lemon wedges and cocktail sauce.

CHICKEN MATTONE
WITH SALTED LEMON

Aside from being one of my favorite foods to make and eat, I love this dish because it makes practical use of the broken pieces of a salt block, as salt blocks eventually break apart after frequent cooking. It is important to place a weight on the chicken to ensure it has complete contact with the salt block during cooking. This allows the skin to render its fat and become crispy. Beware that a little oil is likely going to run off your salt block during cooking so you may prefer to make this in a pan and just use the salt block as a weight.

SERVES 2

PREP TIME: 5 MINUTES,
PLUS 25 MINUTES TO HEAT
THE SALT BLOCK

COOK TIME: 12 MINUTES

4 large boneless, skin-on
chicken thighs

Freshly ground black pepper

Canola oil, for coating the block

2 lemons, halved

1. Gently heat your salt block on the stovetop to medium-high heat, about 25 minutes.

2. Use a paper towel to pat the chicken dry before seasoning it with black pepper. Lightly oil the hot salt block and place the chicken on it, skin-side down. Place several pieces of broken salt block on the chicken as weights to press it down as it cooks. This weight forces all the skin to come in contact with the hot salt block, allowing it to crisp.

3. After about 8 minutes check the chicken skin. When it is golden brown and crispy, remove the weights and turn the chicken. Place the halved lemons, cut-side down, on the salt block as the chicken continues to cook, about 4 minutes more. Once the chicken is cooked through and the skin is crispy, serve it immediately with the lemon halves.

TIP If you don't have any broken pieces of salt block, a heavy cast iron pan works as a great weight. Just remember to clean the bottom of the pan before placing it on the chicken.

PRESSED PROSCIUTTO PANINI

Paninis are Italian sandwiches that are pressed during cooking and served warm. There are many variations to the sandwich, but the basic components are bread, meat, and cheese. Since cured meats and cheese are not seasonal, I know I can enjoy a delicious sandwich year round. But during the summer when tomatoes are at their peak, there are few things better in this world than adding a slice of tomato and a few basil leaves to this sandwich.

SERVES 4

PREP TIME: 10 MINUTES,
PLUS 20 MINUTES TO HEAT
THE SALT BLOCK

COOK TIME: 8 MINUTES

8 (½-inch-thick) slices ciabatta

Extra-virgin olive oil

12 thin slices prosciutto di Parma

2 (4-ounce) balls fresh whole-milk mozzarella, cut into 8 slices total

1. Preheat a salt block on the stovetop to medium heat, about 20 minutes.

2. Drizzle one side of four of the ciabatta slices with the olive oil and place them oil-side down on a cutting board. Place two mozzarella slices on each ciabatta slice, then add three prosciutto slices on top of the cheese. Top each sandwich with another ciabatta slice and drizzle the tops with more olive oil.

3. Place the sandwiches on the hot salt block and place another salt block (or pieces of a broken salt block) on top of them to press them down as they cook. Cook until the bread is golden brown, about 4 minutes. Remove the weight, turn the sandwiches, and return the salt block weight to the top of the sandwiches. Once the second side has browned, about 4 more minutes, transfer the sandwiches to plates, cut them in half, and serve warm.

TIP Since there are so few ingredients in this dish, don't skimp on quality. Finding an Italian market that carries high-quality foodstuffs will help ensure success.

CHICKEN PICCATA
WITH LEMON AND CAPERS

Normally chicken piccata is made in a sauté pan and served with a rich white wine–butter sauce. I've modified the recipe a bit since a considerable amount of liquid would run off the sides of the salt block. The result is a lighter version of chicken piccata, so you'll especially enjoy this recipe if you love the flavors of piccata but not such a rich sauce.

SERVES 2

PREP TIME: 20 MINUTES,
PLUS 30 MINUTES TO HEAT
THE SALT BLOCK

COOK TIME: 6 MINUTES

2 boneless, skinless chicken breasts, butterflied

Sea salt

½ cup all-purpose flour

Canola oil, for coating the block

2 tablespoons unsalted butter, at room temperature

¼ cup capers, drained, chopped, and soaked in water to remove excess brine

¼ cup chopped fresh parsley

½ lemon, plus 2 wedges for garnish

1. Gently heat the salt block on the stovetop to high heat, about 30 minutes.

2. Use a paper towel to pat the chicken dry. Lightly season both sides of chicken with salt. Place the flour in a pie plate and dredge the chicken in it. Brush the hot salt block with oil, shake off any excess flour from the chicken, and place the chicken on the block. Cook the chicken until it is browned on both sides, about 1½ minutes per side. The butterflied chicken is thin, so it will cook very quickly.

3. Transfer the chicken to the serving plates. Working quickly, spread the butter over the hot chicken and add the capers, parsley, and a squeeze of lemon. Gently mix these together with the back of a knife to help the butter melt and create a sauce for the chicken. Serve immediately with a lemon wedge on the side.

TIP If you want a richer dish, make a traditional white wine–butter sauce on the stovetop. In a small saucepan over low heat, combine the butter with ⅓ cup dry white wine and ⅓ cup chicken stock. Stir the sauce occasionally until it has the consistency of heavy cream. Remove the pan from the heat and stir in the parsley and capers.

PORK CHOPS
WITH BUTTERED APPLES

Nothing is more delicious than a simple recipe that tastes complicated. Apples and pork are a classic combination, and the use of a foil package takes advantage of the radiant heat from the salt block. As the salt block heats the foil package, the apples and butter steam, creating a delicious sauce for the pork chops.

SERVES 4

PREP TIME: 10 MINUTES,
PLUS 25 MINUTES TO HEAT
THE SALT BLOCK

COOK TIME: 20 MINUTES

2 crisp apples, peeled, cored, and cut into ¼-inch wedges

½ lemon

3 tablespoons unsalted butter, cut into small cubes

4 center-cut pork chops

Canola oil, for coating the block

1. Gently heat the salt block on the stovetop to medium-high heat, about 25 minutes.

2. While the salt block is heating, layer the apple slices on it and cook them for 1 minute, then turn them and cook for 1 minute more. Place a piece of parchment paper on top of a piece of equal-sized aluminum foil and place the warmed apples in the center of the parchment paper. Squeeze the lemon over the apples and then dot them with the butter. Tightly wrap the apples in the parchment and foil. Press down to compact the apples in as thin a layer as possible, while ensuring a tight seal. If the package is not sealed tightly, the steam from the apples will escape and they will cook too slowly. Place the packaged apples on the hot salt block for 10 minutes. Place the unopened foil package on a serving plate and allow the apples to continue to steam in the foil package.

3. Pat the pork chops dry. Lightly oil the hot salt block and place the chops on it. Cook the pork chops for 4 to 5 minutes per side. Once the pork is cooked through, transfer it to the serving plate. Carefully unwrap the foil package and spoon the apples and their liquid over the pork. Serve immediately.

TIP When selecting apples for this recipe, look for a crisp apple like a Braeburn or Pink Lady; soft apples become mushy as they cook.

BEEF FAJITAS

Sizzling fajitas served in a restaurant is a wow moment. This recipe is a great way to take advantage of the salt block's natural ability to retain heat and makes for a dramatic table presentation at home. Go full salt-block service and serve these fajitas with Salted Lime Guacamole (page 38) and Olive Oil Tortillas (page 54).

SERVES 4

PREP TIME: 10 MINUTES,
PLUS 4 HOURS TO MARINATE,
AND 25 MINUTES TO BRING THE
BEEF TO ROOM TEMPERATURE
AND HEAT THE SALT BLOCK

COOK TIME: 15 MINUTES

2 garlic cloves, minced

1 teaspoon sweet paprika

1 teaspoon ground cumin

3 tablespoons freshly squeezed lime juice

1 (1½-pound) skirt steak, cut against the grain into thin strips

8 flour tortillas

Canola oil

1 yellow onion, halved and thinly sliced

2 bell peppers (any color), cored and cut into thin strips

1. To make the fajita marinade, combine the garlic, paprika, cumin, and lime juice in a large bowl. Add the beef strips to the bowl and toss them to coat in the marinade. Cover the bowl and refrigerate for at least 4 hours, or ideally overnight. Bring the beef to room temperature before cooking it on the salt block.

2. Brush both sides of the tortillas with a small amount of oil. Stack the tortillas on a large piece of aluminum foil and wrap them so they are entirely sealed within the foil package. Place the package on a cold salt block. Place the salt block on the stovetop and heat it to medium-high heat, about 25 minutes. Periodically turn the foil package until the tortillas are warm. Once the outside of the package is hot, remove them from the salt block and set aside.

3. In a medium bowl, toss the onion and bell peppers with enough oil to coat them. Place them on the hot salt block and cook them, stirring occasionally, until they become a little tender but still have a slight crunch, about 6 minutes. Transfer the onion and peppers to a bowl and set aside.

4. Remove the beef strips from the marinade and place them on the hot salt block. Turn the meat frequently until it has fully cooked, about 6 minutes total. Return the onion and peppers to the salt block and cook them with the beef for another minute. Turn off the heat and carefully transfer the salt block with the fajitas to the table, placing the hot block on a trivet. Serve with the warmed tortillas.

TIP Save the marinade and use it as a sauce for the fajitas. Bring it to a boil in a small saucepan, whisk in ½ cup sour cream, season to taste with salt and black pepper, and drizzle it over the beef.

SWEET AND SOUR BEEF

I find that the key to cooking the beef—any protein, really—is keeping it as dry as possible. The salt block does a wonderful job of removing moisture, which helps sear and crisp the outside of the meat. I like to serve this dish with steamed white rice and lots of freshly grated ginger.

SERVES 2

PREP TIME: 10 MINUTES, PLUS 30 MINUTES TO HEAT THE SALT BLOCK

COOK TIME: 5 MINUTES

2 tablespoons low-sodium soy sauce, divided

¾ teaspoon ground ginger, divided

¼ teaspoon freshly ground black pepper

1 pound skirt steak, cut against the grain into thin strips

1 cup water

1 tablespoon cornstarch

3 tablespoons white wine vinegar

3 tablespoons freshly squeezed lemon juice

5 tablespoons sugar

Canola oil, for coating the block

1. Gently heat your salt block on the stovetop to high heat, about 30 minutes.

2. In a large bowl, whisk together 1 tablespoon of soy sauce, ½ teaspoon of ground ginger, and the black pepper. Use a paper towel to pat the beef dry. Add the beef to the bowl and toss it in the mixture to coat the beef strips evenly.

3. To make the sauce, combine the water and cornstarch, and set aside. Mix the vinegar, lemon juice, sugar, remaining 1 tablespoon of soy sauce, and remaining ¼ teaspoon of ground ginger in a saucepan, and bring it to a boil. Remix the cornstarch-water mixture before stirring it into the boiling sauce. Reduce the heat to low and stir until the sauce has thickened, 20 to 30 seconds. Remove the pan from the heat and set aside.

4. Lightly oil the hot salt block. Use a pair of tongs to spread the beef over the oiled salt block in a single layer. Cook the beef strips until cooked through, about 1½ minutes per side. Serve immediately with the warm sweet and sour sauce.

TIP The key to thickening sauces with cornstarch or potato starch is to make sure the sauce is boiling and continually stir it as you stream in the slurry of starchy water.

SEARED RIB EYE
WITH SALT BLOCK GREEN PEPPERCORN SAUCE

Beef and a hot salt block are a match made in heaven. The intense radiant heat of the salt block makes for a wonderful sear on a steak. A thick rib eye is ideal for this recipe so you can get the outside of the steak crunchy without overcooking the meat. I like to cook one or two large steaks, which I then cut into thick slices. Ask your butcher to cut you two 1½-inch-thick steaks from the center of the rib eye for an extra special meal.

SERVES 4 TO 6

PREP TIME: 5 MINUTES, PLUS 30 MINUTES TO HEAT THE SALT BLOCK

COOK TIME: 10 TO 15 MINUTES

2 (1½-pound) boneless rib-eye steaks

Freshly ground black pepper

2 tablespoons minced shallot

1 tablespoon coarsely ground green peppercorns

1. Gently heat a salt block on the stovetop to high heat, about 30 minutes.

2. Pat the rib eyes dry and season them with black pepper. Place the steaks on the hot salt block and sear them for 5 to 8 minutes per side, depending on how well done you like your meat. Remove the steaks to a plate, let them rest for about 5 minutes, and slice and fan the meat on a serving platter.

3. Turn off the heat under the salt block. Add the shallot and green peppercorns to the salt block. Cook them, stirring frequently, for about 2 minutes. Meanwhile, the steak should have released some juice as it rests. Carefully pour 1 to 2 tablespoons of the juice over the shallots and peppercorns, stirring everything to combine. Be careful not to add too much of the juice at once or it will run off the sides of the salt block. The sauce will reduce quickly on the hot salt block, so work fast to combine the ingredients before all the liquid evaporates.

4. Spoon the sauce over the steak slices and serve.

TIP As an alternative to using the steak juices, you can use cognac or brandy. If you are worried about making a mess with the sauce, make it in a saucepan rather than on the salt block. This is a good example of a recipe that benefits from being prepared in a salt block that has pitted slightly in the center.

CHAPTER FIVE

ROASTING AND BAKING

Roasting and baking foods on a salt block may seem a little finicky at first since you have to preheat the block and the oven separately. A preheating oven—especially a gas oven—is at its most humid, and moisture is not the salt block's friend. A salt block can crack or even explode if it takes on too much moisture. To successfully bake and roast on a salt block, first heat the salt block on the stovetop while the oven is preheating (see page 20 for stovetop heating instructions for your salt block). The salt block needs to be the same temperature as the heated oven—or hotter—before the salt block is placed in the oven. Once you do it a few times, you'll get the hang of moving the hot block, and the results will be worth it. The salt block will get very hot in the oven, so you'll definitely want a pair of high-heat silicone oven mitts or heavy kitchen gloves to move the salt block.

I highly recommend putting the block in a salt block holder or on a rimmed baking sheet to catch any spills. This will minimize any mess in your oven and keep rendered fat from hitting the hot oven floor, which will then burn and smoke.

ROASTING AND BAKING TIPS

➡ Position the oven rack toward the bottom of the oven. This will ensure that you have plenty of room to reach into the oven when removing the salt block.

➡ Make sure the salt block and oven are close to the same temperature before placing the block in the oven. Always heat the salt block first on the stovetop before putting it in a fully heated oven. If your oven is not hot enough, it is more likely to be humid and you risk breaking the salt block and potentially damaging your oven.

➡ Use a little oil for moister foods, which are prone to sticking, to grease the salt block. Always oil the salt block when it is hot.

➡ Use the hot salt block's residual heat to keep foods warm at the dinner table. Place the hot block on a trivet to avoid damaging the table surface and then place a dish of hot food on the block. Just keep in mind that the block will continue to cook whatever you place on it if it is significantly hot. And of course be sure to keep it out of the reach of children.

BEETS ROASTED
ON AROMATIC SALT

Roasting beets in rock salt has several things going for it. First, it allows the beets to release more liquid, resulting in a firmer texture. Second, the bottoms of the beets will not burn or scorch as they do when cooked directly on a metal pan. But the biggest upside to this recipe is the aroma from the salt. Make this on a dreary winter day and the lingering spice aromas will make you forget about the world outside.

SERVES 4

PREP TIME: 10 MINUTES,
PLUS 20 MINUTES TO HEAT
THE SALT BLOCK

COOK TIME: 45 MINUTES

2 cups rock salt, roughly
pea-size

1 tablespoon whole fennel seed

1 tablespoon whole allspice

6 whole cloves

6 whole star anise pods

12 medium beets, trimmed

1. Preheat the oven to 400°F. Preheat a salt block on the stovetop to medium heat, about 20 minutes.

2. In a medium bowl, combine the rock salt, fennel seed, allspice, cloves, and star anise. Spread the mixture in an even layer on the hot salt block, roughly ½ inch thick. Place the beets in the salt, pressing them down slightly so they are secure and won't roll off.

3. Carefully transfer the salt block to the oven and roast the beets until a knife pierces each beet with little resistance, about 45 minutes. Peel and quarter each beet and allow to cool slightly before serving. The beets can be eaten as is or marinated in a little olive oil and champagne vinegar.

TIP Save the salt spice mixture to use for future roasting or put it in a hot oven alone to perfume the house. You can even add the used salt mixture to a hot mineral bath.

CELERY ROOT ROASTED
UNDER A SALT BLOCK

In this recipe, the salt block both seasons the celery root and creates a nutty, sweet crust. You can serve the whole celery root rounds as a main course or dice them to make a salad. They are wonderful served with toasted hazelnuts, crème fraîche, freshly ground black pepper, and some fresh thyme leaves.

SERVES 4

PREP TIME: 10 MINUTES, PLUS 20 MINUTES TO HEAT THE SALT BLOCKS

COOK TIME: 30 MINUTES

2 celery root bulbs, scrubbed and cut into 1-inch-thick rounds

Canola oil

1. Preheat the oven to 400°F. Preheat two salt blocks on the stovetop to medium heat, about 20 minutes.

2. Layer the celery root rounds on a baking sheet and lightly drizzle them with oil. Place the hot salt block on top of the celery root. Use a second hot salt block in order to completely cover and weight down the celery root.

3. Carefully transfer the baking sheet to the oven and roast the celery root until very tender, about 30 minutes. Serve immediately.

TIP Leaving the skin on the celery root helps it steam and cook faster. Serve the celery root with the skin on or trim it away if you prefer.

CARROTS ROASTED
WITH HONEY AND ANISE SEED

Naturally sweet carrots are made sweeter with the addition of honey and anise seed. Roasting browns the skins and adds a pleasant bitterness. Head to your local farmers' market and look for young multicolored carrots no bigger than ½ inch in diameter.

SERVES 4

PREP TIME: 5 MINUTES, PLUS 25 MINUTES TO HEAT THE SALT BLOCK

COOK TIME: 30 MINUTES

2 bunches young carrots, unpeeled, tops removed

Canola oil

1 to 2 tablespoons honey, preferably unfiltered

1 tablespoon anise seed

1. Preheat the oven to 375°F. Slowly heat the salt block on the stovetop to medium-high heat, about 25 minutes.

2. Use a kitchen towel to pat the washed carrots dry. Place them in a large bowl and toss them with just enough oil to coat them. Layer the carrots over the hot salt block and carefully transfer the block to a rack in the center of the oven. Roast the carrots until they are tender, about 25 minutes. If you have a convection oven, turn on the fan to help dry out the carrots, which intensifies their flavor.

3. When the carrots are tender, drizzle them with the honey and sprinkle them with the anise seed. Return them to the oven just until they become fragrant, 2 to 3 minutes. Allow the carrots to cool slightly before serving.

TIP Leaving the skins on root vegetables adds earthiness to their flavor. Gently scrubbing the carrots with a damp towel will remove any dirt.

CRISPY POTATO CAKES

Without salt, potatoes are terribly bland. Salt is what makes potato chips and French fries so addictive. In this recipe, the salt from the block seasons the potatoes and makes crispy little hash brown cakes. Make sure to use starchy russet potatoes and rinse them well. I like to use a salad spinner to get them as dry as possible just before cooking.

SERVES 4

PREP TIME: 20 MINUTES, PLUS 1 HOUR TO SOAK

COOK TIME: 30 MINUTES

4 russet potatoes

3 tablespoons canola oil

Freshly ground black pepper

Coarse sea salt

1. Peel the potatoes and shred them on the largest holes of a box grater. For the best results, transfer the shredded potatoes to a bowl of cold water and let them sit in the cold water at room temperature for an hour.

2. Preheat the oven to 375°F. Gently heat a salt block on the stovetop to medium-high heat, about 25 minutes.

3. Drain the potatoes and rinse them under cold running water. After washing out the starch, place the potatoes in a salad spinner to dry or spread them out on a kitchen towel and roll it into a log in order to squeeze out the excess water. In a large bowl, toss the potatoes with the canola oil and season with black pepper.

4. Place ½-cup piles of shredded potatoes on the hot salt block and press them down to flatten them into cakes. Carefully transfer the salt block to the oven. Roast the potato cakes until the bottoms have browned, about 15 minutes. Turn the cakes over and brown the other side, about 15 minutes more. Season the finished potato cakes with coarse sea salt and serve.

TIP Dry potatoes plus a hot salt block will yield crispy edges. The potatoes should give a sizzle and release steam as soon as you add them to the salt block.

SWEET POTATOES
WITH CRÈME FRAÎCHE AND BLACK PEPPER

The natural sweetness of sweet potatoes begs for the contrast that comes from the salt and pepper in this recipe. Sweet potatoes are more nutritious than regular potatoes; they have more nutrients and fewer calories, making them a rare treat among healthy foods.

SERVES 4

PREP TIME: 5 MINUTES,
PLUS 25 MINUTES TO HEAT
THE SALT BLOCK

COOK TIME: 30 TO 40 MINUTES

4 medium sweet potatoes, scrubbed and halved lengthwise

Canola oil

⅓ cup crème fraîche

Freshly ground black pepper

1. Preheat the oven to 400°F. Gently heat a salt block on the stovetop to medium-high heat, about 25 minutes.

2. In a large bowl, toss the sweet potatoes with just enough oil to coat them. Place the hot salt block on a rimmed baking sheet. Place the sweet potatoes cut-side down on the hot salt block. Carefully transfer the baking sheet to the oven. Bake the potatoes until a knife easily pierces through each half, 30 to 40 minutes.

3. Transfer the sweet potatoes to a serving dish, cut-side up. Smash each potato slightly with a fork and allow them to cool for about 5 minutes. Add a dollop of the crème fraîche to each potato, season with a generous amount of black pepper, and serve.

TIP Make sure to leave the skin on the sweet potatoes. Besides being extremely delicious and nutritious, cooking is accelerated if the potato remains in its skin.

CAULIFLOWER "STEAKS"
WITH SICILIAN RAISIN SALSA

Here the salt block adds great depth of flavor to an otherwise mild vegetable. This salsa is so good that I like to increase the recipe size and eat the leftovers by itself or with thick slices of toasted bread.

SERVES 4

PREP TIME: 15 MINUTES, PLUS 30 MINUTES TO HEAT THE SALT BLOCK

COOK TIME: 25 TO 35 MINUTES

Canola oil

4 (1½-inch-thick) slices cauliflower, cut from top to bottom so the core holds each slice together

⅓ cup golden raisins

¼ cup sweet Marsala wine

¼ cup toasted pine nuts

2 tablespoons chopped fresh parsley

½ cup extra-virgin olive oil

Juice of ½ lemon

Freshly ground black pepper

1. Preheat the oven to 350°F. Heat the salt block on the stovetop to high heat, about 30 minutes.

2. With the canola oil, lightly oil both the hot salt block and both sides of the cauliflower slices. Place the cauliflower in a single layer on the salt block. Carefully transfer the salt block to the oven and bake the cauliflower until it is fully cooked and lightly browned, 25 to 35 minutes. If you have a convection oven, turn on the fan a few minutes before the cauliflower is finished to help brown the outside of the slices.

3. While the cauliflower is roasting, make the salsa. Put the raisins in a medium bowl. In a small saucepan, heat the wine just until it begins to boil and then pour it over the raisins. Allow the raisins and liquid to cool. Once cooled, add the pine nuts, parsley, olive oil, lemon juice, and season with black pepper. Stir until well combined. Adjust the seasoning with more lemon juice and black pepper, if necessary. The salsa should be thick but runny, so use less or more olive oil to achieve this.

4. Transfer the cauliflower "steaks" to a serving dish and spoon the salsa over them. Serve immediately.

TIP Don't be afraid of lightly burning the outside of the cauliflower. Allowing the outside to lightly scorch and even get a little black adds a slightly bitter element to the flavor, which pairs great with the sweetness of the salsa.

OVEN-DRIED TOMATOES
IN OLIVE OIL

In late summer, when tomato season is in full swing and you have more than you know what to do with, turn to the salt block. Drying tomatoes on a salt block will draw out their moisture and intensify their sweetness. While any ripe tomato will work, this preparation is ideal with meaty tomatoes that are especially sweet and firm.

MAKES ABOUT 2 CUPS

PREP TIME: 10 MINUTES,
PLUS 25 MINUTES TO HEAT
THE SALT BLOCK

COOK TIME: 1 HOUR

8 ripe tomatoes, about 3 inches in diameter

Canola oil

2 garlic cloves, minced

3 thyme sprigs

Freshly ground black pepper

1 cup extra-virgin olive oil

1. Preheat the oven to 375°F. Slowly heat the salt block on the stovetop to medium-high heat, about 25 minutes.

2. Halve each tomato lengthwise and place them in a large bowl. Add enough canola oil to coat the tomatoes, then add the garlic, thyme, and a few grinds of black pepper and stir to coat the tomatoes.

3. Place the hot salt block on a rimmed baking sheet. Place the tomatoes cut-side down on the salt block and carefully transfer the baking sheet with the salt block to the center rack of the oven.

4. After 30 minutes, turn the tomatoes cut-side up and roast them for another 30 minutes. At the end of the hour, the tomatoes should be about half their original size. Transfer the tomatoes and seasonings to a clean mason jar. Immediately pour in the olive oil. Allow the jar to completely cool before tightly sealing it and refrigerating.

TIP These tomatoes benefit from a day or two of rest before they are eaten. They can be refrigerated for up to a week.

WHOLE FISH
ROASTED IN A SALT CRUST

This dish makes a dramatic presentation for an anniversary or Valentine's Day. Baking fish in a salt crust traps the steam generated from the heat so that the fish cooks gently. The result is a succulent, moist, and flavorful fish that presents beautifully.

SERVES 2

PREP TIME: 20 MINUTES, PLUS 30 MINUTES TO HEAT THE SALT BLOCK

COOK TIME: 30 MINUTES

1 (1½- to 2-pound) whole fish, such as branzino, cleaned but with the head still attached

Sea salt

Freshly ground black pepper

1 lemon, thinly sliced

2 parsley sprigs

2 cups kosher salt

5 to 6 egg whites, beaten

1. Preheat the oven to 425°F. Gently heat a salt block on the stovetop to high heat, about 30 minutes. Place the salt block on a baking sheet and carefully transfer it to the fully heated oven.

2. Use a paper towel to pat the fish dry. Season the inside of the fish with sea salt and black pepper. Overlap a layer of lemon slices inside the fish and place the parsley sprigs on top of the lemon.

3. Put the kosher salt in a large mixing bowl and stir in the egg whites. The mixture should have the consistency of very wet sand.

4. Remove the salt block from the oven and place a thin layer of salt mixture on the salt block to create a bed for the fish. Place the fish in the center of the block. Completely cover the fish with the kosher salt mixture and use a spatula to pack the salt around the fish. Make sure to fill in any gaps so that the fish is completely encased in the salt.

5. Return the salt block to the oven and bake the fish for 30 minutes. The salt crust should be completely set and beginning to brown. Remove the block from the oven and carefully break the salt crust and pull it away from the fish. Serve the fish directly on the salt block.

TIP The recipe itself is fairly simple, but I recommend a practice run before the big day, as there's no better way to know when the fish is done than by trial and error. Generally speaking, by the time the salt crust has fully set, a fish weighing less than 2 pounds will be fully cooked.

SLOW-ROASTED SALMON
WITH WHOLE-GRAIN MUSTARD

There's nothing worse than dry, overcooked fish. But the salt block needs to heat slowly, so that reduces the risk of serving overdone salmon for dinner. While the fish cooks gently, you can make a salad and set the table for an easy dinner with very little prep time or cleanup needed.

SERVES 4

PREP TIME: 10 MINUTES,
PLUS 20 MINUTES TO HEAT
THE SALT BLOCK

COOK TIME: 15 MINUTES

Canola oil, for coating the block

⅓ cup whole-grain mustard

⅓ cup crème fraîche

Freshly ground black pepper

4 salmon fillets, skin on

4 lemon wedges, for garnish

1. Preheat the oven to 350°F and gently heat a salt block on the stovetop to medium heat, about 20 minutes.

2. Place the hot salt block on a rimmed baking sheet and lightly oil the surface of the block.

3. In a small bowl, combine the mustard and crème fraîche and season it with black pepper.

4. Place the fish skin-side down on the salt block and smother the top of each fillet with the mustard sauce.

5. Place the baking sheet on the center rack of the oven. Roast the fish until it has reached the desired level of doneness, about 15 minutes. Place a fillet on each plate and garnish each with a lemon wedge. Serve.

TIP Serving the salmon right on the salt block makes for a special presentation. Experiment with removing the salmon from the oven before it is fully cooked, after 10 to 12 minutes. Allow the residual heat of the salt block to finish cooking the salmon for 5 to 8 minutes. Doing so makes for a supremely delicate texture. If someone wants a piece of fish cooked a little more, just pop the salt block back in the oven for a few more minutes.

TROUT FILLETS ROASTED
WITH ALMONDS AND GREEN BEANS

Trout and almonds is a classic combination. The almonds and green beans give texture to the dish, the lemon brightens the flavors, and the parsley adds freshness. All these elements help elevate the mild taste and texture of trout. This recipe is designed to be cooked and served family-style as part of a multicourse meal. I recommend starting the meal with Celery Root Remoulade (page 45).

SERVES 4

PREP TIME: 15 MINUTES,
PLUS 25 MINUTES TO HEAT
THE SALT BLOCK

COOK TIME: 8 MINUTES

4 trout fillets, skin on

Extra-virgin olive oil

5 tablespoons unsalted
butter, divided

1½ cups thin, tender
green beans

Sea salt

½ lemon plus 4 wedges,
for garnish

⅓ cup sliced almonds

2 tablespoons chopped
fresh parsley

1. Preheat the oven to 350°F. Heat the salt block on the stovetop to medium-high heat, about 25 minutes.

2. Use a paper towel to pat the trout dry and lightly oil both sides of the fillets. Place the fish skin-side down on the hot salt block. Carefully transfer the salt block to the oven.

3. While the fish is roasting, heat a sauté pan over medium-high heat. Melt 1 tablespoon of butter and add the green beans. Season with sea salt. A splash of water to the pan helps steam the beans. (Fresh young green beans are already wonderfully tender, so the pan does not need to be covered while they steam.) Cook the green beans, tossing frequently, until they are tender, about 3 minutes.

4. Take the salt block out of the oven and arrange the green beans on top of the trout fillets. Return the salt block to the oven and continue roasting until the fillets are done, about 8 minutes total. When the trout has finished cooking, place the salt block on a trivet at the table.

5. Return the sauté pan to the stovetop and add the remaining 4 tablespoons of butter, swirling it in the pan until it turns a deep, nutty brown. Squeeze the lemon half into the butter and add the almonds, parsley, and season with sea salt. Swirl everything in the pan to combine before pouring the sauce over the green beans and trout. Serve garnished with the lemon wedges.

SEA BASS WRAPPED IN KELP

In this Japanese-inspired recipe, wrapping the fish in seaweed both seasons the fish and slows the cooking process so the fish doesn't overcook. If you can't find fresh kelp or other seaweed, rehydrate dried seaweed in warm water until it is soft.

SERVES 4

PREP TIME: 10 MINUTES, PLUS 25 MINUTES TO HEAT THE SALT BLOCK

COOK TIME: 15 MINUTES

4 (6-ounce) sea bass fillets, about 1½ inches thick, skin optional

4 tablespoons red miso

4 large pieces kelp or other wide seaweed

4 tablespoons mirin

1. Preheat the oven to 375°F. Slowly heat a salt block on the stovetop to medium-high heat, about 25 minutes.

2. Use a paper towel to pat the fish dry. Spread 1 tablespoon of miso over the top of each fillet. Wrap each fillet in a piece of kelp.

3. Place each wrapped fillet on the hot salt block. Splash each wrapped fillet with 1 tablespoon of mirin. Carefully transfer the salt block to the oven.

4. Roast the fish for 12 to 15 minutes. To check that the fish is cooked through, unwrap one of the fillets. The fish is done if it easily breaks in half. If it is not fully cooked, rewrap that piece and return the salt block to the oven. Carefully unwrap the finished fillets and transfer them to plates. Serve the seaweed alongside the fish as a garnish.

TIP Look for red miso at an Asian food market. You'll be amazed at the options compared to the limited selection at typical grocery stores.

STANDING RIB ROAST

Standing rib roasts are ideal for the winter holidays. When it's cold and dark outside, all you want to do is stay inside and share good food with loved ones. Present the rib roast on a thick salt block and grate a broken piece of salt block over the meat after slicing.

SERVES 4 TO 6

PREP TIME: 10 MINUTES, PLUS OVERNIGHT TO CHILL, AND 25 MINUTES TO HEAT THE SALT BLOCK

COOK TIME: 1½ TO 2 HOURS, PLUS 30 MINUTES RESTING TIME

1 (5-pound) standing rib roast, bones still attached

Sea salt

Freshly ground black pepper

5 garlic cloves, mashed to a paste

1. The day before cooking, pat the roast dry and season the sides with salt and pepper. Rub the roast with the garlic paste and refrigerate it.

2. The next day, bring the roast to room temperature.

3. Preheat the oven to 225°F. Slowly heat a salt block on the stovetop to medium-high heat, about 25 minutes.

4. Place the hot salt block on a rimmed baking sheet. Place the roast on the salt block and carefully transfer it to the oven. Roast for 1½ hours, then check the temperature of the meat. Once the internal temperature reaches 100 degrees the roast's internal temperature will begin to rise much faster. The roast is finished once the internal temperature has reached 125°F. Remove the roast from the salt block and transfer it to a clean baking sheet. Let it rest for 30 minutes; the internal temperature of the roast will rise to 135°F, maximum. Set the warm salt block aside.

5. Once the roast has rested, slice it into thick pieces. Fan out the slices over the warm salt block. Grate a piece of a broken salt block over the meat and serve.

TIP Use an instant-read thermometer to check the internal temperature of the roast.

WARM BRIE
WITH FALL FRUIT

This preparation is a way to use your salt block as a service item. Warm Brie is a delicious appetizer and a perennial guest favorite. Serving it on a warm salt block ensures that the radiant heat from the block keeps the cheese soft and gooey for a long time. Fresh seasonal fruit is a wonderful accompaniment, but your favorite dried fruits can be used as well.

SERVES 4

PREP TIME: 5 MINUTES,
PLUS 25 MINUTES TO HEAT
THE SALT BLOCK

COOK TIME: 6 MINUTES

1 (5-inch) round Brie, at room temperature

1 loaf crusty bread, sliced

Slices of fresh fall fruit such as apples, figs, and pear

1. Preheat the oven to 350°F. Heat your salt block on the stovetop to medium-high heat, about 25 minutes.

2. Place the Brie on the hot salt block. Carefully transfer the salt block to the oven. Bake the Brie until its center is soft to the touch, about 6 minutes.

3. Place the hot salt block on a trivet on the table. Serve immediately with a basket of crusty bread slices and a bowl of sliced fruit.

TIP If the Brie hasn't reached room temperature and you're ready to warm it, wrap it in a piece of parchment paper or aluminum foil before placing it on the hot salt block. Be careful when unwrapping the Brie since it will be very soft.

RYE CRACKERS
WITH SALT BLOCK GRAVLAX AND CRÈME FRAÎCHE

After you've made your own Dill-Cure Salmon Gravlax (page 123), prepare these simple crackers, and you can quickly put together a delicious appetizer the next time you have guests. You can make the crackers a day ahead of time and store them wrapped in plastic or in an airtight container.

SERVES 8 TO 10

PREP TIME: 30 MINUTES,
PLUS 1 HOUR TO REST

COOK TIME: 10 MINUTES
PER CRACKER

1 cup rye flour

1 cup all-purpose flour, plus additional for dusting

1 teaspoon salt

3 tablespoons extra-virgin olive oil

⅔ cup warm water

8 ounces Dill-Cured Salmon Gravlax (page 123), thinly sliced

Crème fraîche

Freshly ground black pepper

1. In a standing mixer fitted with a dough hook attachment, combine the rye and all-purpose flours and the salt. Add the olive oil to the cup with the warm water and, with the mixer running at low speed, slowly stream the oil and water into the flours until a dough ball forms and there is no dough clinging to the sides of the bowl. The dough should be soft but should not stick to your fingers. Increase the mixer speed to medium and continue mixing the dough for 7 minutes. Wrap the dough in plastic wrap and let it rest for 1 hour.

2. Preheat the oven to 375°F. Slowly heat a salt block on the stovetop to medium heat, about 20 minutes.

3. Cut the dough into four equal-size pieces and cover three of them with plastic wrap. Place the fourth piece on a lightly flour-dusted wooden cutting board and lightly dust the top of the dough piece with flour. Use a rolling pin to roll out the dough as thin as possible. (A hand-crank pasta roller will make quick work of this, if you have one.) Lightly dust flour on the dough as you roll it out to prevent it from sticking. Brush off any excess flour and place the dough on the hot salt block. Carefully place the salt block in the oven and bake the cracker until it is crisp, about 10 minutes. Repeat this process with the remaining dough pieces.

4. Once the large crackers have cooled, break them into smaller pieces. Place a dollop of crème fraîche on the cracker, followed by a slice of gravlax. Top with dill and a few grinds of black pepper. Serve.

TIP When using hard flours like wheat or rye, make sure to use at least an equal amount of all-purpose flour, too. The all-purpose flour helps make a softer dough, which is easier to roll.

MELTED RACLETTE
WITH PICKLES AND LITTLE POTATOES

Raclette is a semi-soft cow's milk cheese from the Alps. Traditionally, a large wedge is heated until it starts to melt, and it's then scraped onto a plate and served alongside potatoes and salty foods like pickles and ham. Here, the salt block melts the cheese and celebrates the tradition of the salty accompaniments. Think of this dish as fondue without the pot.

SERVES 4

PREP TIME: 10 MINUTES, PLUS 20 MINUTES TO HEAT THE SALT BLOCK

COOK TIME: 16 MINUTES

16 new potatoes, such as butterball or fingerling, scrubbed

Olive oil

Sea salt

1 (10-ounce) wedge Raclette, at room temperature

1 cup cornichon pickles

8 ounces sliced ham

1 loaf fresh crusty bread, sliced

Freshly ground black pepper

1. Preheat the oven to 375°F. Gently heat a salt block on the stovetop to medium heat, about 20 minutes.

2. Meanwhile, put the potatoes in a saucepan and cover with cold water. Set the pan over medium-high heat and bring the water to a boil. Reduce the heat to a simmer and cook the potatoes until very tender, about 10 minutes. Transfer the potatoes to a bowl and coat them lightly with olive oil and sea salt.

3. Place the wedge of Raclette on the hot salt block. Carefully transfer the salt block to the oven. After about 3 minutes, use a spatula to turn the cheese to accelerate the melting. The cheese is ready once the edges have browned slightly and it is soft enough to spread with a knife, about 3 minutes more.

4. While the Raclette is in the oven, divide the potatoes (halved if larger than 1 inch in diameter), pickles, ham, and bread slices among four plates.

5. Scrape the melted cheese onto the plates and lightly season with black pepper. Serve immediately.

TIP The cheese pairs wonderfully with a Riesling or Pinot Gris wine. Any dry white wine with high acidity will work well, but wines from the French and Swiss Alps are best.

RICOTTA AND SPINACH FLATBREAD

This flatbread is more like a thick cracker than a bread, so it works well as a base for hors d'oeuvres or just as a snack. The recipe makes a fair amount of dough, so I like to leave some of the baked crackers plain and save them for later. Wrap them tightly in plastic wrap and they will keep well for several days.

SERVES 4

PREP TIME: 30 MINUTES,
PLUS 1 HOUR TO REST

COOK TIME: 15 TO 20 MINUTES
PER FLATBREAD

1 cup whole-wheat flour

1 cup all-purpose flour, plus
more for dusting

2 teaspoons sea salt

5 tablespoons extra-virgin
olive oil, divided

¾ cup warm water, about 100°F

2 bunches spinach (about
1 pound)

1 recipe Fresh Ricotta Aged on
a Salt Block (page 125)

Freshly ground black pepper

1. In a standing mixer fitted with a dough hook attachment, combine the whole-wheat and all-purpose flours and the salt. Add 3 tablespoons of olive oil to the cup with the warm water and, with the mixer running at low speed, slowly stream the oil and water into the flours until a dough ball forms and there is no dough clinging to the sides of the bowl (you may not need all the water). The dough should be soft but should not stick to your fingers. Increase the mixer speed to medium and continue mixing the dough for 7 minutes. Wrap the dough in plastic wrap and let it rest for 1 hour.

2. Preheat the oven to 375°F. Slowly heat a salt block on the stovetop to medium heat, about 20 minutes.

3. In a large skillet, heat the remaining 2 tablespoons of olive oil over medium-high heat. Add the spinach and toss with tongs until it wilts, 3 to 5 minutes. Chop the spinach and set aside. ➡

4. Cut the dough into four equal-size pieces and cover three of them with plastic wrap. Place the fourth piece on a lightly flour-dusted wooden cutting board and lightly dust the top of the dough piece with flour. Use a rolling pin to roll out the dough to roughly ⅛-inch thickness, dusting the rolling pin and the dough with flour as necessary to prevent the dough from sticking. Brush off any excess flour and place the dough on the hot salt block. Carefully place the salt block in the oven and bake the flatbread until it is crisp, 15 to 20 minutes. Remove the flatbread from the salt block and allow it to cool. Repeat this process with the remaining dough pieces.

5. Break the cooled flatbread into pieces. Spread the ricotta on the cracker pieces, top each with some of the spinach, and season with black pepper. Serve.

TIP You can add more flavors to the flatbread in any number of ways. Here's one idea: Once the flatbread has crisped in the oven, brush it with warm honey and sprinkle it with anise seeds. Return the salt block to the oven and bake the flatbread for an additional 2 to 3 minutes.

SALTED BUTTERMILK BISCUITS
WITH HONEY AND BUTTER

There's perhaps no better way to start the weekend—or any morning, if I'm honest—than with a warm buttermilk biscuit fresh from the oven. You can make and refrigerate the dough the evening before so that you can have a more relaxing morning. Baking the biscuits on a salt block gives the bottoms a unique salty crust.

MAKES 12 BISCUITS

PREP TIME: 30 MINUTES,
PLUS 20 MINUTES TO HEAT
THE SALT BLOCK

COOK TIME: 15 MINUTES

3 cups all-purpose flour, plus additional for dusting

4 teaspoons baking powder

2 teaspoons sea salt

1 teaspoon baking soda

1½ cups (3 sticks) cold unsalted butter, cut into small cubes

1 cup cold buttermilk

¼ cup heavy (whipping) cream

Honey, preferably unfiltered, for serving

Salted butter, at room temperature, for serving

1. Preheat the oven to 375°F. Slowly heat a salt block on the stovetop to medium heat, about 20 minutes.

2. In a large bowl, combine the flour, baking powder, salt, and baking soda. Add the butter cubes and incorporate them into the dry ingredients by smashing and crumbling them with your fingers. Working quickly to avoid melting the butter with your hands, mix the dough until it resembles coarse sand with occasional bits of butter. Do not overmix the dough. Use a wooden spoon to stir the buttermilk into the dough. Once it is combined, lightly flour your hands and mix the dough for 30 seconds to make sure the ingredients are evenly incorporated.

3. Place the dough on a lightly flour-dusted wooden cutting board and dust the top of the dough with additional flour. Gently roll out the dough to form a rectangle about 1½ inches thick. Use a sharp knife to cut the rectangle into 12 squares. Place the biscuits on a baking sheet and then place the baking sheet in the freezer for 10 minutes to chill. After 10 minutes, brush the biscuits with the heavy cream.

4. Remove the biscuits from the baking sheet and place them directly on the hot salt block. Carefully transfer the salt block to the oven and bake the biscuits until they are golden brown, about 15 minutes.

5. Serve warm with honey and butter.

TIP The key to fluffy biscuits is incorporating the cold butter into the dough without melting it and not overworking the dough. I also like to freeze the biscuits briefly before baking them; I find this makes for a lighter biscuit.

PIZZA
ON A SALT BLOCK

Salt blocks are thicker and denser than most pizza stones, so they work even better at transferring even, radiant heat to the bottom of the pie. Since you probably don't have a circular salt block, you'll need to either make small rectangular pizzas or place two salt blocks together to create a large enough surface for one round or large rectangular pie. The salt block is also ideal for warming up leftover pizza or even baking a premade frozen pizza.

MAKES 2 MEDIUM PIZZAS

PREP TIME: 30 MINUTES, PLUS 1 HOUR TO RISE

COOK TIME: 12 TO 15 MINUTES PER PIZZA

2½ teaspoons (1 package) active dry yeast

1½ teaspoons sugar

1 cup warm water, about 100°F

2 cups all-purpose flour, plus more for rolling out the dough

2 teaspoons sea salt

Canola oil

Tomato sauce

Fresh mozzarella cheese, broken into pieces

⅓ cup grated Parmesan cheese

1. In a small bowl, dissolve the yeast and sugar in the warm water. Let the mixture stand for 5 minutes.

2. In the bowl of a standing mixer fitted with a hook attachment, combine the flour and salt. With the mixer on low speed, slowly stream the water mixture into the flour until it forms a dough ball. You may not need all the water (see Tip). The dough will be soft but should not stick to your fingers or to the sides of the bowl. Oil a large bowl and place the dough ball in it. Cover the bowl with plastic wrap and set it aside in a warm place to rise. The dough should rise to double its volume, about 1 hour.

3. About 30 minutes before the dough finishes rising, preheat the oven to 400°F and slowly heat the salt block(s) on the stovetop to high heat, about 30 minutes. Carefully transfer the hot salt block to the center rack of the oven.

4. After the dough has doubled in volume, punch it down and divide the dough into the number of pizzas you plan to make. Place one dough ball on a lightly flour-dusted wooden cutting board or a pizza peel, if you have one. Stretch the dough or use a rolling pin so that it is no more than ¼ inch thick and will just fit on your salt block. Add more flour to the cutting board if the dough is sticking.

5. Spoon a thin layer of tomato sauce onto the dough. Arrange 6 to 8 pieces of mozzarella on the surface of the pie and then sprinkle the whole pizza with the Parmesan.

6. Pick up the cutting board or peel and give it a light shake to make sure the pizza is not sticking to the surface. Open the oven and carefully slide the pizza onto the salt block. Bake the pizza until the cheese is melted and the edges of the crust are browned, 12 to 15 minutes. Repeat this process for any remaining dough pieces. Serve.

TIP Use your own judgment regarding how much yeasty water to add when making the dough. The dough should be soft and slightly sticky without any residual dough clinging to the outside of the mixing bowl.

NAAN
WITH TIKKA MASALA

The radiant heat of the salt block allows the naan to puff up and bake without burning on the outside. Wrap any extra naan in plastic and freeze. Place a piece of frozen naan on the salt block while it preheats and let it cook for about 5 minutes per side.

MAKES 12 LARGE PIECES

PREP TIME: 1 HOUR,
PLUS 1½ HOURS TO RISE

COOK TIME: 8 MINUTES PER BATCH

2½ teaspoons (1 package) active dry yeast

5 tablespoons sugar

1 cup warm water, about 100°F

1 tablespoon sea salt

¼ cup milk

1 egg, beaten

4½ cups all-purpose flour, plus more for rolling out the dough

Canola oil

3 tablespoons unsalted butter, melted

Tikka masala spice blend

1. In a medium bowl, dissolve the yeast and sugar in the warm water. Let it stand for 5 minutes. Stir in the salt, milk, and egg. Put the flour in the bowl of a standing mixer fitted with a dough hook. On low speed, add the yeast mixture to the flour, which will form a soft dough. Transfer the dough to a lightly floured surface and knead it with your hands until it is smooth and elastic, 5 to 8 minutes. Oil the inside of a large bowl and the outside of the dough ball and place the dough in the bowl. Cover the bowl with plastic wrap and set it aside in a warm part of the kitchen until the dough has doubled in volume, about 1 hour.

2. Preheat the oven to 375°F. Slowly heat a salt block on the stovetop to medium-high heat, about 25 minutes.

3. Once the dough has doubled in volume, punch it down. Tear off 12 pieces of dough and roll them into balls about 1½ inches in diameter. Place the balls 2 inches apart on an oiled baking sheet. Cover the sheet with plastic wrap and set it aside in a warm place. The dough balls should rise until they have doubled in volume, about 30 minutes.

4. Using a rolling pin, roll out each ball to about ¼-inch thickness; they will be about 6 inches in diameter. Lightly dust the rolling pin and the surface of the dough with some flour if the dough sticks to the surface. Place one piece of rolled-out dough on the hot salt block and carefully transfer the salt block to the oven. Bake the naan until it is lightly browned and puffy, about 4 minutes per side. Brush the naan with some melted butter and sprinkle with tikka masala. Repeat with the remaining dough. These naan are best eaten warm.

TIP Although this recipe is designed for the oven, you can also make the naan on the stovetop or grill. If grilling over charcoal, partially cover the grill in order to trap the smoke, which in turn flavors the naan.

BILLIONAIRE'S BACON

Who knew bacon could be made even more delicious? Coating slices of bacon in brown sugar and caramelizing it in the oven may be over the top, but it's wildly delicious. This recipe is simple and will yield a salty snack that will delight all bacon lovers.

SERVES 8

PREP TIME: 10 MINUTES,
PLUS 25 MINUTES TO HEAT
THE SALT BLOCK

COOK TIME: 15 MINUTES

1 pound neutral-flavored smoked bacon, sliced

1¼ cups brown sugar

1. Preheat the oven to 400°F. Slowly heat a salt block on the stovetop to medium-high heat, about 25 minutes.

2. Lay the strips of bacon on a paper towel and dry both sides. Sprinkle the brown sugar evenly over both sides of the bacon, pressing firmly to the bacon so it sticks. Don't worry that some sugar will fall off.

3. Place the hot salt block on a rimmed baking sheet. Place the bacon strips on the salt block and carefully transfer it to the oven. Bake until the sugar is browned and caramelized and the bacon is crispy, about 15 minutes.

4. Transfer the bacon to a nonstick surface to cool a bit. Serve.

TIP This is a messy dish. Make sure to place a baking sheet under the salt block to catch the molten pork fat and sugar that will drip off the sides of the block while it cooks.

CHAPTER SIX
GRILLING

Charcoal grilling is my favorite way to cook with a salt block. The food is seasoned by the salt block and then gains more flavor from the smoke generated by the burning coals. Foods that release a lot of fats and juices during cooking are ideal for the grill—think steaks, hamburgers, and sausages. As fat renders and drips off the sides of the salt block, it hits the hot coals and creates smoke, which in turn flavors the food. It's perfect symmetry.

Begin heating the coals on one side of the grill and place the salt block on the grill grate on the other side. As the coals get hotter and the salt block begins to heat, gradually move the block closer to the hot embers. When both are hot, spread the burning coals across the entire bottom of the grill.

Gas grills are even easier for salt blocking cooking. Just as on a gas stovetop, the salt block can be heated slowly as the gas grill heats. (It is much harder to control the temperature of a charcoal grill.)

Because heating a salt block on the grill is a tricky process, I strongly recommend starting your salt block grilling experience by heating it first on the stovetop and moving it to the grill once both are hot. As you become more comfortable with salt block grilling, you can experiment with heating the salt block right on the grill. It will take time and practice to get it right.

GRILLING TIPS

➡ Just as with stovetop or oven cooking, the salt block needs to be heated gradually. Placing a cold or room-temperature block on a hot grill threatens the integrity of the block and increases the risk of breakage.

➡ When cooking vegetables on the grill, toss them in a little oil before placing them on the hot salt block. The oil increases the heat transfer to the food and provides a better sear, which results in more flavor.

➡ After cooking on the salt block on the grill, I like to move foods directly onto the grill for a few moments to incorporate more smoke. You can also infuse smoke by moving the salt block to one side of the grill once you've finished cooking. Close the lid on the grill and let the food pick up the residual smoke from the dying embers.

➡ For even smokier foods, soak some wood chips in water and toss them onto the hot coals. Just be careful not to create too hot an environment inside the grill or you'll risk overcooking and drying out your food.

➡ Smaller foods that usually fall through the gaps in a grill grate are ideal for salt block grilling. Start them directly on the grill to get a little extra color and smoke on them, then transfer them to the salt block before they significantly shrink.

➡ Cool the salt block on the grill. The salt block is going to take several hours to cool, so leave it on the grill overnight and clean it in the morning.

LEEKS
WITH ANCHOVY-LEMON DRESSING

Leeks vinaigrette is a classic French dish for a simple reason: It is easy to make and delicious. Typically, leeks are boiled until they are soft and then served with an acidic dressing. But by cooking them on a salt block on the grill, they will steam and soften without losing as much flavor as when boiled.

SERVES 4

PREP TIME: 15 MINUTES, PLUS 20 MINUTES TO HEAT THE SALT BLOCK

COOK TIME: 20 MINUTES

10 young leeks, about 1 inch in diameter

Canola oil

8 salt-packed anchovy fillets, such as Agostino Recca

2 hard-cooked eggs, chopped

½ cup extra-virgin olive oil

Juice of 2 lemons

Freshly ground black pepper

1. Preheat the grill and a salt block to medium heat, about 20 minutes. If using a charcoal grill, spread the hot coals evenly around the bottom of the grill. Position the block over the hottest portion of the grill.

2. Trim the top 1 to 2 inches of dark green tops from the leeks. Remove the outer layer of each leek and cut them in half lengthwise. Thoroughly wash them to clean out the dirt that is between the layers. Lightly oil the leeks and place them cut-side down on the hot salt block. After about 8 minutes, flip the leeks and continue cooking until they are tender, 5 to 8 minutes longer.

3. While the leeks are grilling, make the dressing. On a cutting board, mince the anchovies into a paste and transfer this to a small bowl with the chopped eggs. Add the olive oil and lemon juice, and season with black pepper. Stir until well combined. Adjust the seasoning if necessary.

4. Once the leeks are tender, place them directly on the hottest portion of the grill for 2 to 3 minutes to gain some color, turning them frequently. Once they are slightly charred, transfer them to a platter and drizzle with the dressing. Serve immediately.

TIP Keep the leeks as close together as possible on the salt block so they steam each other slightly. Don't be afraid to pile them on top of each other. Just make sure to periodically mix them around so they cook evenly. You don't have to put the leeks on the grill at the end, but it does add nice color and an extra depth of flavor.

GRILLED HEARTS OF ROMAINE LETTUCE

For a full salt block meal, serve this grilled romaine with Whole Chicken Grilled under a Salt Block (page 109) or Lamb Kebabs with Harissa (page 114). Perhaps you'll even want to make a salt block dessert or cocktail to enjoy as well.

SERVES 4

PREP TIME: 5 MINUTES,
PLUS 25 MINUTES TO HEAT
THE SALT BLOCK

COOK TIME: 2 MINUTES

4 romaine hearts, halved lengthwise

Extra-virgin olive oil

4 Black Pepper–Cured Egg Yolks (page 124)

1 lemon

Freshly ground black pepper

1. Preheat the grill and a salt block to medium-high heat, about 25 minutes. If using a charcoal grill, spread the hot coals evenly around the bottom of the grill.

2. Drizzle the romaine hearts with olive oil and arrange them very close together, cut-side down, on the grill. Place the hot salt block on top of the lettuce. Crowding the lettuce together plus the weight of the salt block help the romaine steam and cook. After 2 minutes, the outside of the romaine will be slightly burned; it will be soft on the outside but still crunchy inside.

3. Place the romaine on a serving platter and grate the cured egg yolks over the lettuce. Season with a healthy squeeze of lemon juice and a few grindings of black pepper. Serve.

ZUCCHINI
WITH BASIL AND PINE NUTS

Come summer, zucchini is rarely in short supply. There's only so much zucchini you can give away before your friends start to avoid you, so this is a great recipe to add to your repertoire. It can be eaten right off the grill or stored in the refrigerator for another day. It only gets better as the flavors marry.

SERVES 4

PREP TIME: 10 MINUTES, PLUS 25 MINUTES TO HEAT THE SALT BLOCK

COOK TIME: 15 MINUTES

½ cup extra-virgin olive oil, plus additional to brush the zucchini

2 medium zucchini, cut lengthwise into ½-inch-thick slices

1 garlic clove

1 cup tightly packed fresh basil leaves

¼ cup toasted pine nuts

¼ cup grated Parmesan cheese

Freshly ground black pepper

1. Preheat the grill and a salt block to medium-high heat, about 25 minutes. If using a charcoal grill, spread the hot coals evenly around the bottom of the grill. Position the hot salt block over the hottest portion of the grill.

2. Lightly oil the zucchini slices and place them in a single layer on the hot salt block. Turn the zucchini after about 5 minutes. Continue to cook until they become slightly tender, about 2 minutes more.

3. While the zucchini is cooking, make the pesto. Put the garlic in a mortar and smash with the pestle. Add the basil leaves and pound them into the garlic until a paste forms. Add the pine nuts and grind them just enough to break them into pieces. Stir in the Parmesan and ½ cup of olive oil.

4. Once the zucchini has barely cooked through, transfer it to a serving platter. Drizzle the pesto over the zucchini and season everything with black pepper. Serve immediately, or cool and store in the refrigerator.

TIP Make mortaring easier by giving ingredients a coarse chop before pounding. Adding a pinch of salt will also help. You can alternatively make the pesto in a food processor if you want, but you should still mortar the garlic.

WILTED KALE
WITH PARMESAN AND LEMON

Grilling is all about simple cooking. Here the salt block protects the kale from the fire so that it has time to cook and does not burn. Move the kale back and forth between the salt block and the grill grate as it cooks to control the amount of char the edges of the kale take on. This dish is delicious eaten by itself or added to hamburgers and other sandwiches.

SERVES 4

PREP TIME: 5 MINUTES,
PLUS 25 MINUTES TO HEAT
THE SALT BLOCK

COOK TIME: 10 TO 15 MINUTES

2 bunches kale (about 1 pound), stems removed

Extra-virgin olive oil

½ cup grated Parmesan cheese

Chili flakes

Juice of ¼ lemon

1. Preheat the grill and a salt block to medium-high heat, about 25 minutes. If using a charcoal grill, spread the hot coals evenly around the bottom of the grill. Position the hot salt block over the hottest portion of the grill.

2. Toss the kale with olive oil and place it on the hot salt block for about 5 minutes. Transfer the kale to the hot grill, making sure not to let the kale burn, about 2 minutes. Alternate between the salt block and the grill a few times, until the kale is tender and slightly charred.

3. Place the kale on a cutting board and chop it. Return the chopped kale to the salt block and mix it with the Parmesan cheese, a pinch of chili flakes, and the lemon juice. Once everything is well mixed, place the kale on a serving dish and serve.

TIP Feel free to double the recipe. The greater the volume of greens, the easier they cook because more leaves allow for more steam to wilt them.

SMOKY EGGPLANT DIP

This dish is a perfect way to use the cooling embers of a charcoal grill. As the grill starts to cool, place several whole eggplants directly in the coals to slowly bake. The thick skin traps the steam generated inside the eggplant and cooks it while also taking on a smoky flavor from the coals. Partially cooking the eggplant on the salt block reduces the intensity of the smoky flavor. Make this dip as an appetizer for a meal later in the evening or even the next day—store it in an airtight container in the refrigerator.

SERVES 4

PREP TIME: 20 MINUTES,
PLUS 25 MINUTES TO HEAT
THE SALT BLOCK

COOK TIME: 20 MINUTES

3 small Japanese eggplants

Cayenne pepper

Extra-virgin olive oil

Crackers, for serving

1. Preheat a charcoal grill and a salt block to medium-high heat, about 25 minutes. Keep the hot salt block off to the side of the grill while you grill other foods. Once finished grilling, wait for the coals to cool down a bit, about 15 minutes, and then place the eggplants directly on the coals. Turn the eggplants after 5 minutes and cook for 5 minutes more.

2. Remove the eggplants from the coals and cut them in half lengthwise—be careful as they will release hot steam when they are cut. Place the eggplant halves cut-side up on the warm salt block and transfer the block to the coolest part of the grill. Cover the grill for 10 minutes.

3. Remove the eggplant halves from the salt block and scrape the flesh back onto the reserved hot salt block. Sprinkle the eggplant with some cayenne pepper. Use a rubber spatula to slowly mix in the olive oil. Stop mixing once the eggplant cannot absorb any more oil. Transfer the dip to a serving bowl and let it cool. Serve with crackers.

TIP Look for eggplants that are heavy for their size. Small, dense eggplants are meatier and have better flavor.

WHOLE TROUT
WRAPPED IN PANCETTA

Trout is mild in flavor so there's no reason not to use a heavy hand when seasoning it. Stuff the fish with loads of herbs and Salted Meyer Lemons (page 129), wrap it in pancetta, and let the salt block do the rest. The fish cooks gently, so there's no need to stress about grill flare-ups from the rendering pancetta fat.

SERVES 4

PREP TIME: 20 MINUTES, PLUS 25 MINUTES TO HEAT THE SALT BLOCK

COOK TIME: 20 MINUTES

½ cup chopped fresh parsley

2 tablespoons fresh thyme leaves

2 tablespoons diced Salted Meyer Lemons (page 129)

½ cup coarse bread crumbs

4 whole trout, semi-boneless

16 thin strips pancetta

1. Preheat the grill and a salt block to medium-high heat, about 25 minutes. If using a charcoal grill, spread the hot coals evenly around the bottom of the grill. Position the hot salt block over the hottest portion of the grill.

2. In a medium bowl, combine the parsley, thyme, Meyer lemons, and bread crumbs. Use a paper towel to pat the trout dry and stuff each fish with an equal amount of the herb mixture.

3. On a cutting board, lay 4 strips of the pancetta parallel to one other. Place a trout crosswise in the middle of the pancetta and loosely wrap the strips around the mid-section of the fish. Repeat this process with the remaining pancetta and trout.

4. Place the pancetta-wrapped trout on the salt block. Adjust the heat of the grill so the pancetta gently sizzles but does not burn. Once the pancetta begins to crisp, about 8 minutes, turn the fish. Move the salt block to a cooler portion of the grill if necessary to slow the cooking process, and cover the grill. After another 8 minutes, check the inside of the fish to ensure it is done. Serve immediately.

TIP As the pancetta renders and crisps, it will shrink around the fish. Avoid wrapping the pancetta too tightly around the fish. This may cause it to break away from the trout when you turn it or at the end of cooking when you remove it from the salt block.

SWEET GINGER SALMON

Salmon cooked on a charcoal grill is delicious hot or cold, so you might consider doubling the recipe right off the bat. Eat the hot salmon over rice with Japanese Cucumber Salad (page 128) for dinner, then have the leftovers the following day for lunch over a salad. Do you like crispy salmon skin? Just before the salmon has cooked through, place it skin-side down directly on the grill grate for the last minute or two of grilling.

SERVES 4

PREP TIME: 15 MINUTES,
PLUS 25 MINUTES TO HEAT
THE SALT BLOCK

COOK TIME: 8 MINUTES

2 tablespoons grated
fresh ginger

1 garlic clove, minced

1 tablespoon brown sugar

1 tablespoon low-sodium
soy sauce

4 (6-ounce) center-cut salmon
fillets, skin on

Canola oil

1 cup wood chips, soaked in
water for 5 to 10 minutes

1. Preheat a charcoal grill and a salt block to medium-high heat, about 25 minutes. Spread the hot coals evenly around the bottom of the grill. Position the hot salt block over the hottest portion of the grill.

2. In a small bowl, combine the ginger, garlic, brown sugar, and soy sauce to form a loose paste. Add a little water if necessary.

3. Use a paper towel to pat the fish dry. Brush the skin side with canola oil. Place the fillets skin-side down on the hot salt block. Spoon the ginger glaze over each fillet.

4. Toss the wood chips over the hot coals and cover the grill to trap the smoke. When the fish is cooked through, about 8 minutes, transfer it to a serving plate. Serve immediately.

TIP Smoking is a great way to add flavor to food when grilling. This recipe doesn't work as well on a gas grill as the smoking wood chips make a terrible mess and are difficult to clean up.

LOBSTER TAIL
GRILLED IN ITS SHELL

It's not every day that you eat lobster, so it's all the more reason to make a special occasion of it. Here, by butterflying the tail and cooking it in its shell, the meat cooks slowly in between the shell and the radiant heat of the salt block. The claws do not have enough contact with the salt block to cook properly, so it's best to prepare them separately.

SERVES 4

PREP TIME: 20 MINUTES,
PLUS 25 MINUTES TO HEAT
THE SALT BLOCK

COOK TIME: 20 MINUTES

4 live Maine lobsters

½ cup (1 stick) unsalted
butter, melted

1. Preheat the grill and a salt block to medium-high heat, about 25 minutes. If using a charcoal grill, spread the hot coals evenly around the bottom of the grill. Position the hot salt block over the hottest portion of the grill.

2. Use a very sharp knife to split each lobster in half lengthwise, being careful to leave the two sides of the tail shell partially attached. (If you're squeamish about cutting into a live lobster, you can first kill it by putting it in the freezer.) Gently separate the tails from the bodies and set them aside.

3. Remove the claws and knuckles from the bodies. Each lobster has a dominant claw, which is larger. In a pot of salted water over the lowest heat possible, simmer the larger claws for 8 minutes and the smaller claws and knuckles for 7 minutes. Drain and cool the claws on a baking sheet.

4. While the claws are cooling, brush each butterflied tail with some of the melted butter and place them cut-side down on the hot salt block. Cook the tails until the meat has turned from opaque to white and has firmed, about 3 minutes. The meat will continue to cook slightly in its shell once it's removed from the salt block, so don't be afraid to remove the tails a little earlier than you might think (see Tip).

5. Brush each lobster tail with more melted butter and serve with the warm lobster claws and the remaining melted butter.

TIP Lobster tails cook quickly and become tough and chewy if overcooked. Don't worry about removing them from the salt block too early—you can always return them to the hot salt block if they are not quite done.

WHOLE CHICKEN
GRILLED UNDER A SALT BLOCK

Spatchcocking is a centuries-old method of cooking poultry. By removing the backbone and laying the bird flat, the cooking time is greatly reduced and it is easier to carve the bird once it is cooked. The name may be odd, but spatchcocking is easy to do. Lay the bird breast-side down on a cutting board. Using sharp kitchen scissors, make two cuts running vertically along both sides of the backbone and remove the backbone. Push down on the sides of the bird and spread it out flat. In this recipe the salt block acts more as a weight than as a seasoning since the unevenness of the bird limits the amount of contact it has with the salt block.

SERVES 4

PREP TIME: 10 MINUTES, PLUS 20 TO 25 MINUTES TO HEAT THE SALT BLOCK

COOK TIME: 40 MINUTES

1 tablespoon sugar

2 tablespoons sea salt

2 tablespoons sweet paprika

1 tablespoon smoked paprika

2 teaspoons freshly ground black pepper

1 teaspoon cayenne pepper

1 whole chicken, spatchcocked

1. If using a gas grill, preheat the grill and a salt block to medium heat, about 20 minutes. Or, if using a charcoal grill, preheat the grill and the salt block to medium-high heat, about 25 minutes. Arrange the hot coals in a ring around the perimeter of the grill, slightly larger than the size of the chicken, leaving a few coals scattered in the center of the ring.

2. In a small bowl, combine the sugar, salt, sweet and smoked paprikas, black pepper, and cayenne pepper. Use a paper towel to pat the chicken dry. Evenly season both sides of the bird with the seasoning mixture.

3. Place the chicken on the center of the grill grate, skin-side down, and place the hot salt block on top of it.

4. Check the chicken periodically to ensure that it is not taking on color too fast. If it is, adjust the coals, pushing them farther away from the chicken. After 15 to 20 minutes the bird will have taken on an even, dark color. Remove the salt block weight and turn the bird over. Return the salt block to the top of the bird and cook the chicken for 15 to 20 minutes more. Once the thighs are completely cooked, remove the chicken from the grill. Carve the bird and serve.

TIP If you are concerned that the breasts will overcook, remove them from the legs once they are finished and keep them warm while the legs and thighs finish grilling.

TEA-SMOKED DUCK BREAST

If you've never had tea-smoked duck, you're in for a treat. Added bonus: It is delicious either hot or cold. The duck is cooked directly on the charcoal grill and then rested on the salt block while it is tea smoked. The salt block transfers very little salt to the duck, so make sure to season it well before cooking. If you can't find duck breasts, chicken works well, too.

SERVES 4

PREP TIME: 10 MINUTES, PLUS
1 TO 2 HOURS TO MARINATE

COOK TIME: 20 MINUTES

4 boneless duck breasts, trimmed of excess fat, skin scored

Sea salt

Freshly ground black pepper

2 garlic cloves, mashed to a paste

1 tablespoon grated fresh ginger

2 tablespoons extra-virgin olive oil

1 tablespoon brown sugar

1 tablespoon uncooked rice

1 tablespoon loose black tea leaves

1. Season the duck breasts with sea salt and black pepper.

2. In a large bowl, combine the garlic, ginger, and olive oil to make a marinade. Toss each breast in the marinade until it is coated. Cover the bowl with plastic wrap and set aside at room temperature for 1 to 2 hours.

3. Preheat a charcoal grill. Arrange the hot coals in a ring around the perimeter of the grill so that the center of the grill has low heat.

4. Place the duck breasts on the grill, skin-side down. The fat will render slowly and the skin will become crisp, about 7 minutes. Move the coals farther to the outside of the grill if the rendered fat flares up.

5. Once the skin is crispy, turn the breasts and continue grilling them for 1 minute. Move the coals to one side of the grill and place a room-temperature salt block as far from the coals as possible. Place the cooked breasts skin-side down on the salt block.

6. Form a little cup with some aluminum foil. Add the sugar, rice, and black tea leaves to the foil cup. Stir a few hot coals into the cup to begin burning the tea and place the cup on the salt block next to the duck breasts. Cover the grill and close the vents to trap the smoke inside. Rest the duck breasts for 10 minutes in the smoky grill. Then slice the duck and serve.

TIP If you're concerned with the grill flaring up and burning the duck, cook the breasts directly on the salt block rather than on the grill. Make sure that the block is at a low heat so that the fat has time to slowly render from the duck. This will take an additional 2 to 3 minutes to cook the breasts and the skin will not crisp up as well as it will if cooked on the grill.

BUTCHER'S CHOICE STEAK
WITH ROSEMARY SALT

Next time you're at the meat counter contemplating dinner, let the butcher choose your steak. Ask for a 1½-pound steak to grill and trust the butcher's choice. All steaks cook differently, so ask the butcher for cooking recommendations. Since you'll be grilling a large steak, only the outside will be seasoned, here with a rosemary salt. You can make a flavored salt with nearly any savory herb. It takes just a few days to dry and is easy to make in larger quantities to be stored for a future use.

SERVES 2–4

PREP TIME: 10 MINUTES, PLUS 1 TO 2 DAYS TO DRY THE SALT AND 25 MINUTES TO HEAT THE SALT BLOCK

COOK TIME: 12 TO 18 MINUTES

Leaves from 2 rosemary sprigs

1 cup salt, such as Maldon or fleur de sel

1 (1½-pound) steak, at room temperature

Canola oil, for coating the block

1 lemon, quartered, for garnish

1. Mince the rosemary leaves or pulse them in a food processor. In a small bowl, combine the rosemary and the salt. Spread the salt in a shallow dish to a thickness of about ½ inch and set it aside to dry, uncovered, for 1 to 2 days.

2. Preheat the grill and a salt block to medium-high heat, about 25 minutes. If using a charcoal grill, spread the hot coals evenly around the bottom of the grill. Position the hot salt block over the hottest portion of the grill.

3. Season both sides of the steak with the rosemary salt. Lightly oil the salt block and place the steak on it. Cook the steak according to the butcher's suggestions and transfer it to a cutting board. Larger pieces of meat benefit from resting to avoid releasing greater amounts of liquid. I recommend letting the steak rest for 5 to 10 minutes before slicing it.

4. Thinly slice the meat against the grain, season it with a sprinkle of rosemary salt, and fan the meat on a serving platter. Place a dish of the rosemary salt and the lemon wedges on the table to be used as a garnish. Serve.

TIP Resting larger cuts of meat is very important. If you slice the meat straight from the grill, it will lose a great deal of its juices and flavor, not to mention making a mess. This is true of poultry as well. Use this resting time to toss a salad together.

LAMB KEBABS
WITH HARISSA

Harissa is a sweet-spicy condiment used in North African cuisine. If you're new to harissa, you'll find yourself wanting to keep a batch of it in your refrigerator to drizzle over all sorts of grilled meats, rice, and vegetables for an extra kick of flavor.

SERVES 4

PREP TIME: 15 MINUTES, PLUS 25 MINUTES TO HEAT THE SALT BLOCK

COOK TIME: 10 MINUTES

½ teaspoon cumin seed

½ teaspoon coriander seed

½ teaspoon fennel seed

2 tablespoons sweet paprika

2 tablespoons smoked paprika

1 teaspoon freshly ground black pepper

½ teaspoon cayenne pepper

½ teaspoon sea salt

2 garlic cloves, mashed to a paste

Extra-virgin olive oil

1 (1-pound) boneless lamb leg, cut into 1-inch cubes

1. Preheat the grill and a salt block to medium-high heat, about 25 minutes. If using a charcoal grill, spread the coals evenly around the bottom of the grill. Position the hot salt block over the hottest portion of the grill.

2. In a shallow pan, toast the cumin, coriander, and fennel seed over medium heat until they are fragrant, 1 to 2 minutes. Grind the seeds in a spice grinder or mortar and pestle, and place the mixture in a large bowl. Add the sweet and smoked paprikas, black pepper, cayenne pepper, salt, and garlic. Stir in enough olive oil to make a loose paste that coats the back of a spoon.

3. Transfer half of the harissa to a small bowl and set aside. Add the lamb cubes to the harissa remaining in the large bowl. Toss the cubes in the harissa to coat them. Skewer the lamb on bamboo skewers, pushing the cubes close together so that there are no gaps.

4. Place the lamb kebabs on the salt block, leaving a slight gap between each skewer. Cook the kebabs until the lamb is fully cooked, about 5 minutes per side. Place the kebabs on a serving platter and spoon the reserved harissa over them. Serve immediately.

TIP Pimentón de la Vera is a type of smoked paprika that is remarkably fragrant and smoky, which gives harissa tremendous depth. You can find this spice at nearly any specialty cooking store.

LAMB CHOPS
WITH GREEN OLIVE TAPENADE

In the middle of the summer, the last thing you want to do is heat the house while you prepare dinner. Instead, cook this meal outside while enjoying a glass of chilled wine or a cold beer. Relax and enjoy the warm summer evening.

SERVES 4

PREP TIME: 15 MINUTES, PLUS 25 MINUTES TO HEAT THE SALT BLOCK

COOK TIME: 6 MINUTES

1 tablespoon diced shallot

1 tablespoon champagne vinegar

Canola oil, for coating the salt block

16 center-cut lamb chops

½ cup firm green olives, pitted

1 tablespoon diced Salted Meyer Lemons (page 129)

4 lemon wedges, for garnish

1. Preheat the grill and a salt block to medium-high heat, about 25 minutes. If using a charcoal grill, spread the hot coals evenly around the bottom of the grill. Position the hot salt block over the hottest portion of the grill.

2. Meanwhile, combine the diced shallot and the champagne vinegar in a small bowl and set aside to macerate for at least 15 minutes. Drain the shallot and return it to the bowl, then set aside.

3. Lightly oil the salt block and place the lamb chops on the hot salt block. Cook the chops for 3 minutes on each side.

4. While the lamb is cooking, add the olives and lemon to the bowl with the macerated shallot.

5. Transfer the cooked lamb chops to a large serving platter and cover them with the olive tapenade. Serve with lemon wedges as a garnish.

TIP Avoid frenched lamb chops. The meat between the bones is delicious, so you lose both quantity and flavor if this meat is removed. Don't be afraid to use your fingers to pick up the chops—and don't forget to lick your fingers clean!

FENNEL AND GARLIC PORK SAUSAGE HOAGIES

If you have trouble cooking sausages without splitting the casing, this recipe is a great fix. The sausages are cut in half and cooked directly on the salt block, which means they cook faster and you don't need to worry about the grill flaring and scorching the meat. Toast a few hoagie rolls while the sausages cook and there's little else you need other than mustard and a cold beer.

SERVES 4

PREP TIME: 5 MINUTES,
PLUS 25 MINUTES TO HEAT
THE SALT BLOCK

COOK TIME: 5 MINUTES

Canola oil

4 large fennel and garlic pork sausages, halved lengthwise

4 hoagie rolls

Mustard

1. Preheat the grill and a salt block to medium to medium-high heat, about 25 minutes. If using a charcoal grill, spread the coals evenly around the bottom of the grill. Position the hot salt block over the hottest portion of the grill.

2. Lightly oil the salt block and place the sausages on the block, cut-side down. Cook until they are lightly browned, about 3 minutes. Turn the sausages and cook until they are cooked through, about 2 minutes more.

3. While the sausages are cooking, split the rolls and place them on the grill, cut-side down, to toast. Place the finished sausages in the toasted rolls, give each sausage a generous amount of mustard, and serve.

TIP If you like the crunch of sauerkraut on your sausages, make some Celery Root Remoulade (page 45) and use it to garnish the sausages.

PORK MEDALLIONS
WITH GARLIC AND SAGE

This simple recipe is full of flavor thanks to the garlic and sage. By cooking the tenderloin as a roast on a salt block, you are less likely to overcook the meat. The salt block gives the outside of the pork a salty crust while the interior will be tender and juicy. For an even richer dish, double the amount of sage and garlic and simmer the extra amount in ½ cup heavy cream until the liquid has slightly reduced. Add some lemon juice and spoon this sauce over the pork.

SERVES 4

PREP TIME: 15 MINUTES, PLUS OVERNIGHT TO MARINATE

COOK TIME: 10 MINUTES, PLUS 10 MINUTES TO REST

2 tablespoons dry white wine

2 tablespoons extra-virgin olive oil

3 garlic cloves, mashed to a paste

8 fresh sage leaves, minced

1 (1¼-pound) pork tenderloin

Sea salt

1. In a small bowl, combine the wine, olive oil, garlic, and sage. Use a paper towel to pat the pork tenderloin dry and then rub the seasoning paste over it. Wrap the tenderloin in plastic and refrigerate overnight.

2. Preheat the grill and a salt block to medium-high heat, about 25 minutes. If using a charcoal grill, spread the coals evenly around the bottom of the grill. Position the hot salt block over the hottest portion of the grill.

3. Place the pork on the salt block and sear it for 5 minutes on each side. The outside should be browned and the loin will have a slight resistance when gently squeezed.

4. Transfer the pork to a cutting board and let it rest for 10 minutes. Thinly slice the tenderloin, season it with sea salt, and serve.

TIP The tapered "tail" of the tenderloin will cook much faster than the rest of the loin, so serve this portion to anyone who likes their pork well-done.

DOUBLE PANCETTA CHEESEBURGERS
PRESSED UNDER A SALT BLOCK

There's nothing like a double cheeseburger when you're really hungry. Grill and assemble the burgers and then place them back on the grill over low heat with a broken piece of salt block as a weight. This will toast the bun and compress the burgers, making it easier to take a satisfying bite. This recipe is not for the faint of heart.

SERVES 4

PREP TIME: 15 MINUTES,
PLUS 25 MINUTES TO HEAT
THE SALT BLOCK

COOK TIME: 10 MINUTES

1½ pounds ground beef
(20 percent fat)

8 slices 30-Day Pancetta
(page 134) or bacon

4 hamburger buns

8 slices Cheddar cheese

1. Preheat the grill. If using a charcoal grill, evenly spread the coals in the center of the bottom of the grill.

2. While the grill is heating, form 8 thin hamburger patties slightly larger than the diameter of the buns.

3. Place the pancetta slices on a cooler area of the grill and crisp both sides, 1 to 2 minutes total. Set them aside. Place the hamburger patties on the grill, pressing down on each one as they grill. After 2 minutes, flip the patties and continue to grill them until completely cooked through, another 2 minutes or so. Transfer the patties to a plate.

4. Assemble the burgers by placing a hamburger patty on the bottom of a bun. Add a slice of Cheddar on top of the patty, followed by 2 strips of pancetta. Top the pancetta with another slice of cheese and then a second patty. Place the top of the bun on the hamburger. Repeat this process with the other three hamburgers.

5. Check the temperature of the grill. The heat should be very low now; adjust the coals if necessary to lower the heat level. Place the hamburgers on the grill and place one or more room-temperature salt blocks on top of the burgers, acting as a weight. Once the bottoms of the buns are toasted, about 1 minute, remove the weight, flip the burgers, and toast the top buns, about 1 minute more. Serve.

BEEF SKEWERS
WITH MUSHROOMS

Grilling skewers on a salt block rather than directly on the grill works well because you don't have to worry about flare-ups or having the wooden skewers burn. You can skewer any combination of meat and vegetables, but my favorite is beef and mushrooms. These skewers require very little prep, so you spend more time relaxing by the grill than working in the kitchen.

SERVES 4

PREP TIME: 15 MINUTES,
PLUS 1 HOUR TO MARINATE

COOK TIME: 15 MINUTES

⅓ cup white wine

⅓ cup extra-virgin olive oil

2 garlic cloves, mashed to a paste

1 teaspoon brown sugar

1 pound lean beef, cut into 1-inch cubes

8 ounces cremini mushrooms

1. Combine the white wine, olive oil, garlic, and sugar in a large bowl. Add the beef cubes and mushrooms to the bowl and toss them to coat with the marinade. Cover with plastic wrap and let the beef and mushrooms marinate at room temperature for 1 hour.

2. While the beef marinates, preheat the grill and a salt block to medium-high heat, about 25 minutes. If using a charcoal grill, arrange the hot coals in a ring around the perimeter of the grill slightly larger than the salt block, leaving a few coals scattered in the center of the ring. Place the salt block on the grill grate in the center of the ring.

3. Skewer the beef and mushrooms on bamboo skewers, alternating a beef cube and a mushroom.

4. Place as many skewers on the block as possible without allowing them to touch each other. Cook the skewers until the beef is fully cooked, about 7 minutes total, turning occasionally. Transfer the skewers to a warm place and grill any remaining skewers. Serve immediately.

TIP The rigid stems of an overgrown rosemary bush work great in place of bamboo skewers. Cut 8-inch sections of rosemary and strip the stems of all the leaves except the top 1inch. Cut the bottom of the stem on an angle to make skewering easier.

CHAPTER SEVEN

CURING

Curing food is all about preserving it. As water is removed from a piece of food and salt is introduced, the food becomes less hospitable to bacteria. Of course, there is a wide range of how cured you want a food. Sometimes, as with vegetables, a quick cure is ideal since you just want to draw out moisture and add a little salt to intensify a food's flavor. Other times, as with pancetta, you want a high level of salt and a low level of moisture in order to create an intense flavor and keep the food from spoiling.

The transfer of salt into foods provides the opportunity to introduce other flavors into the food as well. Curing foods on the salt block creates a natural brine. Coating the ingredients you are curing with spices or placing a few herbs on the salt block with them introduces and intensifies the flavors.

Quick-cured items like Mushroom Conserva (page 130) and Japanese Cucumber Salad (page 128) are delicious on their own, as the cure that takes place is subtle, but other items like 30-Day Pancetta (page 134) and Salted Meyer Lemons (page 129) are too salty and intense to eat alone. Saltier cured items such as these are best sliced or diced small and used as an ingredient within a dish. Use these intense items as seasoning to add salt and flavor depth to dishes.

CURING TIPS

➡ Lesser-grade salt blocks are perfect for curing. Since the salt block won't be heated, there's no concern about cracks that could cause the block to break. Also, there's no need for a thick salt block when curing. As a result, salt blocks used for curing cost significantly less than those used for cooking or presentation.

➡ Put your salt block on a rimmed baking sheet to catch the released liquids and reduce mess.

➡ Cut foods thinly and in uniform sizes to both speed up the curing process and ensure that the food cures evenly.

➡ Sandwich foods between two salt blocks. This speeds up the process and helps create a more uniform piece of food.

➡ Check foods regularly when curing them. As foods sit in contact with the salt block, they release liquid, which in turn increases the absorption of salt into the food. This cycle continues until either the block and food item reach equilibrium or the item cannot release any more moisture, at which point most foods have become too salty and dry to be palatable.

➡ Curing improves the texture of foods. As foods dry they becomes denser, firmer, and more concentrated in flavor.

DILL-CURED SALMON GRAVLAX

Gravlax should be the first curing recipe you try. It's very easy to make and is ready to eat in about a day, depending upon the thickness of the fish. Use the freshest wild salmon possible and ask for a center-cut fillet. Once you've made your own gravlax, you'll never want to buy it again. Two salt blocks are needed here.

MAKES ABOUT 1½ POUNDS

PREP TIME: 10 MINUTES

CURE TIME: 1 DAY

¼ cup sugar

1 teaspoon ground coriander

1 teaspoon freshly ground black pepper

1 teaspoon fennel seed, cracked

1 (1½-pound) wild salmon fillet, skin on, pin bones removed

3 tablespoons chopped fresh dill

1. Combine the sugar, coriander, black pepper, and fennel seed in a small bowl. Use a paper towel to pat the fish dry. Evenly cover the skin side of the fillet with the spice mixture.

2. Place a room-temperature salt block on a rimmed baking sheet to catch any liquid released by the fish. Sprinkle half of the dill on the salt block and place the fish, skin-side down, on top of the dill. Sprinkle the remaining dill on top of the fish and place a second room-temperature salt block on top of the fish. The top salt block should be large enough to cover the whole fish.

3. Place the baking sheet in the refrigerator. Allow 1 day for a 1-inch-thick fillet to cure. A thicker fillet will need a little longer under the salt blocks. The gravlax is done when the outside is dry and the flesh is firm to the touch. Once cured, tightly wrap the gravlax in plastic wrap and refrigerate. Gravlax will keep in the refrigerator for up to 1 week.

TIP If you have only one salt block, you're still in luck. Sprinkle ¼ cup sea salt on the skin side of the fish and place the salt block on top of the fish's flesh side, and a rimmed baking sheet beneath. Once the fish is cured, rinse off any excess salt and use a paper towel to pat the gravlax dry before eating or storing it.

BLACK PEPPER–CURED EGG YOLKS

I first ate cured egg yolks grated over pasta. The yolks had a similar texture and richness to cheese and were unexpectedly delicious. By curing egg yolks, they turn into a delicious garnish that can be used nearly any way you may want to use grated cheese: over pastas, in salads, or with vegetables.

MAKES 12 YOLKS

PREP TIME: 20 MINUTES

CURE TIME: 1 DAY, PLUS
1 DAY TO REST

1 ½ cups sea salt

1 cup sugar

12 egg yolks

Freshly ground black pepper

1. In a medium bowl, combine the salt and sugar. Place a room-temperature salt block on a rimmed baking sheet. Spread a very thin layer of the salt mixture over the salt block. Carefully place the egg yolks on the salt, about ¼ inch apart. Season the egg yolks with black pepper, and completely cover with the remaining salt mixture.

2. Transfer the baking sheet to the refrigerator. After 24 to 36 hours, the yolks will become firm disks. Gently rinse them with water. Use a paper towel to pat the yolks dry and place them on a wire rack at room temperature for 1 day. Once they are firm and no longer feel tacky, individually wrap them in parchment paper and store them in the refrigerator for up to 2 months.

TIP   The salt allows the black pepper to be absorbed into the yolks as they cure. You can replace the black pepper with any flavoring agent you want to impart to the yolks. I like fennel seed and floral teas like hibiscus.

FRESH RICOTTA
AGED ON A SALT BLOCK

This is less a way to actually age the cheese and more a way to use the cold salt block to chill the hot cheese while also drawing-out moisture and adding seasoning. Regardless, it's delicious served with bread, crackers, or raw vegetables. I also like it topped with honey and cracked black pepper, or with marmalade. The ricotta is best eaten as fresh as possible, but it can be stored in a covered container in the refrigerator for a day or two.

MAKES ABOUT 1½ CUPS

PREP TIME: 20 MINUTES,
PLUS 2 HOURS TO CHILL
THE SALT BLOCK

CURE TIME: 1 HOUR

2 quarts whole milk

1 cup heavy (whipping) cream

½ cup freshly squeezed
lemon juice

1. Chill the salt block in the freezer for at least 2 hours or overnight.

2. Combine the milk and cream in a large pot and place it on the stovetop over medium heat. Just before the milk begins to boil (between 180°F and 190°F), stir in the lemon juice and turn off the heat. Within a minute, the milk will begin to separate and the curds will rise to the top. Strain the curds through a fine-mesh sieve or a double layer of cheesecloth. Cool and reserve the liquid for another use (see Tip). Leave the curds in the strainer and allow it to drain and dry out until it is roughly the consistency of soft oatmeal, about 30 minutes. ➡

3. Place the chilled salt block on a rimmed baking sheet, then spread the cheese across the surface of the block. As the cheese slowly takes on the salt from the block, it will release more liquid, which will run off the sides of the salt block. Occasionally stir the cheese with a rubber spatula so that it is consistently seasoned and check it for seasoning. Once the ricotta has taken on your desired level of salt, 15 to 20 minutes, serve.

TIP Save the whey (the liquid strained from the cheese). It is mild in flavor and very healthy. You can use it in place of stock for braising meats or making soup. It is also a great substitute for milk when making smoothies.

QUICK PICKLED EGGPLANT CAPONATA

Caponata is a traditional Sicilian dish made of eggplant, celery, and capers. The balance of sweet and sour is what makes caponata so irresistible. In this version, the salt block helps draw out the eggplant's bitterness. If you generally find eggplant too bitter for your taste, try leaving it on the salt block even longer.

MAKES ABOUT 1½ CUPS

PREP TIME: 20 MINUTES, PLUS 2 HOURS TO REST

COOK TIME: 10 MINUTES

1 large globe eggplant, peeled and cut into ¼-inch-thick slices

1 cup extra-virgin olive oil, plus some for coating the pan

1 cup chopped, drained fresh tomatoes

½ yellow onion, finely diced

1 celery stalk, finely diced

2 tablespoons coarsely chopped Sicilian olives

2 tablespoons pine nuts

1 tablespoon chopped capers

1 tablespoon sugar

2 tablespoons freshly squeezed lemon juice or white wine vinegar

Freshly ground black pepper

1. Layer the eggplant slices on a room-temperature salt block and allow them to sit for 30 minutes. Turn the eggplant slices and allow them to sit until tender, another 30 minutes or so.

2. Use a paper towel to pat the eggplant dry and transfer it to a cutting board. Roughly chop the eggplant, and transfer it to a sauté pan with a little olive oil over high heat. Add the tomatoes, onion, and celery and simmer for 10 minutes.

3. Remove from the heat and add the eggplant mixture to a medium mixing bowl with the olives, pine nuts, capers, sugar, 1 cup of olive oil, and the lemon juice and mix everything together well. Season with black pepper.

4. Set the bowl aside and allow it to marinate at room temperature, uncovered, for 1 hour. Check the seasoning and add more sugar or lemon juice if necessary. Serve, or refrigerate until serving time.

TIP This caponata is best after a day or two, giving the flavors time to develop, so make it ahead if possible. Serve with crusty bread as an afternoon snack or as an appetizer before a meal.

JAPANESE CUCUMBER SALAD

Making this cucumber salad on a salt block speeds the process of marrying the flavors. You can make the salad entirely with cucumbers or add zucchini and scallions if you want to mix things up. Regardless of how you make it, you'll always feel as if you haven't made enough.

MAKES ABOUT 2 CUPS

PREP TIME: 15 MINUTES

CURE TIME: 30 TO 60 MINUTES

2 English or Armenian cucumbers, thinly sliced (see Tip)

1 tablespoon sugar

1 teaspoon grated fresh ginger

2 tablespoons rice wine vinegar

1 tablespoon mirin

½ teaspoon toasted sesame oil

Sesame seeds, for garnish

1. Combine the cucumbers, sugar, ginger, vinegar, mirin, and sesame oil in a large bowl. Spread the cucumbers evenly on a room-temperature salt block, reserving any residual liquid in the bowl. Cure the cucumbers on the salt block until they are slightly soft, 30 to 60 minutes.

2. Place the cucumbers back in the bowl with the reserved liquid, stir to mix, garnish with the sesame seeds, and serve.

TIP   Use a mandoline or vegetable peeler to slice the cucumber into thin coins.

SALTED MEYER LEMONS

Salted Meyer lemons are one of those ingredients that once you use it, you cannot live without it. They have a salty intensity that brightens dishes and takes them to an entirely new level. A little goes a long way, so dice them as small as possible before adding them to a recipe. They are delicious in salsas and sauces or added in the final moments of sautéing vegetables. The more you make these lemons, the more uses you will discover.

MAKES ABOUT 1 ½ CUPS

PREP TIME: 20 MINUTES

CURE TIME: 2 DAYS, PLUS
2 TO 4 WEEKS

5 large Meyer lemons, cut into
⅛-inch-thick slices

2 teaspoons fennel seed

2 teaspoons freshly ground
black pepper

2 star anise pods

1 dry bay leaf

¼ cup sea salt

3 tablespoons sugar

½ cup freshly squeezed
lemon juice

1. Place a room-temperature salt block on a rimmed baking sheet. Spread out the lemon slices in a single layer on the salt block. You may need more than one salt block, depending upon the size of the salt block and the lemon slices. Place the baking sheet in the refrigerator and cure the lemon slices for 24 hours. Turn the lemon slices and continue curing them for another 24 hours.

2. In a small bowl, combine the fennel seed, black pepper, and star anise. Pack the lemons in a mason jar while evenly layering the spices throughout. Add the bay leaf, salt, and sugar to the top of the jar and pour in the lemon juice. Tightly seal the jar and refrigerate it for at least 2 weeks. If the rinds are still firm, let them cure for another week or two.

TIP These lemons only get better with time. After a few months the lemons become extremely soft, with an intoxicating aroma.

MUSHROOM CONSERVA

This is my favorite pre-dinner snack. In the spring and fall I love to hunt mushrooms with my daughters. We pick far more than we could possibly eat fresh, so the rest are given to friends or are conserved. We eat these pickled mushrooms during the long periods when wild mushrooms are not available. Any firm, meaty mushroom works well for this recipe. My favorites are porcini and lobster mushrooms, but you can also use cultivated mushrooms like cremini or portobello. I like to wait at least a week before eating them. Feel free to adjust the ratio of salt and vinegar to your own tastes.

MAKES 1 QUART

PREP TIME: 90 MINUTES

CURE TIME: 1 WEEK

1 pound mushrooms, such as porcini or lobster, cut into ½-inch-thick slices

1 quart water

¾ cup champagne vinegar

½ cup sea salt

2 tablespoons sugar

1 tablespoon whole fennel seed

1 tablespoon black peppercorns

2 dry bay leaves

Extra-virgin olive oil

1. Place the mushrooms on a room-temperature salt block and let them sit at room temperature until they start to give off their liquid and shrink a little (this may be hard to see), about 25 minutes. Turn the mushrooms over and continue curing them for 20 minutes more.

2. While the mushrooms are curing, make the brine. Combine the water, vinegar, salt, sugar, fennel seed, black peppercorns, and bay leaves in a stockpot and bring to a boil, then reduce the heat to a simmer. Once the mushrooms have cured on the salt block for about 45 minutes, transfer them to the pot. Simmer the mushrooms in the brine for 3 minutes, then strain the mushrooms and spices from the liquid.

3. Immediately pack the mushrooms and spices in a mason jar. Pour in enough olive oil to cover the contents of the jar. Tightly seal the jar and let the mushrooms cool to room temperature. Store the jar in the refrigerator for 1 week before eating. The flavors will continue to develop the longer the mushrooms rest; they can be enjoyed for a month or more.

TIP Save the olive oil from the mason jar after you eat the mushrooms. It is delicious in salad dressings or as a finishing oil to drizzle over cooked meats. The oil is also amazing as a substitute for butter on popcorn.

KOMBU-CURED MACKEREL

If you're a fan of stronger-flavored, oily fish, then this recipe is for you. Kombu is an edible seaweed, and it adds a fresh essence of the ocean to the mackerel while keeping the fish from taking on too much salt from the block. The fish is delicious simply served over rice with pickled vegetables.

MAKES 2 FILLETS

PREP TIME: 10 MINUTES

CURE TIME: 12 HOURS

2 (4- to 6-ounce) mackerel fillets, skin on

1 tablespoon grated fresh ginger

1 teaspoon sugar

2 large pieces kombu or other wide seaweed

3 tablespoons mirin

1. Place a room-temperature salt block on a rimmed baking sheet to catch any run-off liquid.

2. Use a paper towel to pat the fish dry. Season the fillets with the ginger and sugar. Loosely wrap each fillet in a piece of kombu and place each wrapped fillet on the salt block.

3. Sprinkle the mirin over the wrapped fish. Place the baking sheet in the refrigerator and cure the fish for 12 hours. The fish is ready when the flesh is firm to the touch and has turned opaque.

TIP If you cannot find fresh seaweed, rehydrate dried kombu in warm water until it is soft and pliable.

CITRUS-CURED SALMON

This recipe is very similar to making gravlax except the cure time is shorter, resulting in softer slices of salmon. You can use nearly any type of citrus for this cure. When ready to serve this salmon, use a very sharp, thin-bladed knife to slice the fish. My favorite way to eat this is over shaved fennel tossed in lemon juice and extra-virgin olive oil. You will need two salt blocks.

MAKES ABOUT 1½ POUNDS

CURE TIME: 8 HOURS

1 (1½-pound) wild salmon fillet, skin on, pin bones removed

Zest of 2 limes

Zest of 2 lemons

Zest of 2 oranges

¼ cup sugar

1. Place a room-temperature salt block on a rimmed baking sheet to catch any liquid the salmon releases while it cures.

2. Use a paper towel to pat the salmon dry. Place the fish skin-side down on the salt block. Evenly sprinkle the citrus zests over the fish, then sprinkle the sugar over the fish. Place a second room-temperature salt block on top of the salmon. Place the baking sheet in the refrigerator.

3. Check the fish after 6 hours. The skin should be slightly firm but still bouncy. Gently wipe the sugar from the fish and give it a quick rinse under cool water. Use a paper towel to pat the fish dry. Return the salmon to the salt block and let it air-dry in the refrigerator for 2 more hours.

4. The salmon can be eaten right away or wrapped in plastic wrap and stored in the refrigerator for up to 2 days.

TIP Given many variables, including the airflow within your refrigerator and the thickness of the salmon fillet, cure times will vary. Ultimately, the fish is ready when it reaches your desired level of firmness. The more often you make this, the better you'll be able to refine the timing.

30-DAY PANCETTA

You may be reluctant to make your own cured pork products, but once you taste this recipe you won't want to eat store-bought pancetta again. Here, the salt block is used more as a secondary seasoning agent and as a weight so that the pancetta is pressed flat, making it easier to remove the skin from the final product. There are two essential components to curing pancetta: very fresh, skin-on pork belly, and curing salt (Insta Cure #1). I find that most butcher shops will happily give you a little curing salt so that you don't have to buy a large package. (Note that curing salt is also known as "pink salt," but it is *not* the same thing as the Himalayan pink salt, which is used for seasoning! Curing salt has added nitrites and can be toxic if used in large quantities, so be sure to use only 1/2 teaspoon for this recipe.)

MAKES ABOUT 2 POUNDS

PREP TIME: 15 MINUTES

CURE TIME: ABOUT 30 DAYS

1/4 cup sea salt

1 tablespoon freshly ground black pepper

1 tablespoon fennel seed, cracked

1/2 teaspoon chili flakes

1/2 teaspoon curing salt, such as Insta Cure #1

1 (3 1/4-pound) pork belly, skin on, from the front section of the pig

1 tablespoon mashed garlic

1/3 cup dry white wine

1. In a small bowl, combine the sea salt, black pepper, fennel seed, chili flakes, and curing salt. Use a paper towel to pat the pork belly dry, then season both sides with the curing mixture. Place the pork belly skin-side down in a glass or ceramic baking dish. The dish must be nonreactive, so do not use a metal pan.

2. In a small bowl, stir the garlic into the white wine and pour it over the pork belly. Refrigerate the pork belly, uncovered. After 5 days turn the pork belly over; it will have released a bit of liquid. Continue to refrigerate the pork and check it again in another 5 days. The goal is for the liquid the pork belly is sitting in to evaporate. The timing depends on how well air circulates in your refrigerator, so this process can be faster or slower than expected—it usually takes me about 15 days for the liquid to evaporate. At this point the meat can be eaten or you can continue to dry the panchetta in the refrigerator if you want it firmer. Allowing the panchetta to dry more will make cutting it easier.

3. Once the majority of the liquid has evaporated, place a room-temperature salt block over the pork belly, making sure all of the pork is weighted down and covered by the block, and return it to the refrigerator. Let the pork continue to cure for 15 more days and then slice a small piece from the edge to check for doneness. The meat should be very firm throughout. In addition, the pork will have lost about one-third of its original weight during the curing process.

4. Wrap the finished pancetta tightly in plastic wrap and store it in the refrigerator. The skin is best removed as portions of the pork are served. Use a sharp knife to remove the thick layer of skin from the portion you are using. The pancetta can be kept, tightly wrapped so it doesn't dry out, in the refrigerator for up to a month or in the freezer for even longer.

TIP Using the salt block yields a saltier and more intense pancetta than what's commercially available, so make sure to slice it very thinly or dice it small when using it as an ingredient in another recipe. A little goes a long way.

CHAPTER EIGHT

SWEETS

Salt is a key component in flavoring savory foods, but people often forget the importance of salt in desserts. Sweets benefit from a touch of salt; it enhances the flavors of the other ingredients in the dessert. Chocolate is a great example—a little finishing salt on a piece of chocolate amplifies the cocoa. Without salt, peanut butter cups would lack the sweet and salty balance that makes them so addictive. Remember that salt actually increases the mouth's perception of sugar.

My favorite desserts to make on the salt block are those that benefit from the addition of salt, especially those that include chocolate and peanut butter.

DESSERT TIPS

➡ You can bake sweets on your salt block. Baking desserts like tarts on a salt block allows for even drying of the crust so that the bottom of the tart becomes crisp and evenly browned.

➡ A hot salt block imparts very little salt to the dessert as long as the food is not wet. Keep desserts dry when in contact with the salt block. Avoid serving desserts on a salt block unless the dessert is completely dry.

➡ A pastry chef uses a marble block to cool things like melted chocolate. A salt block works in a very similar way. The block's density mimics that of a slab of marble, enabling you to rapidly cool foods. A hot caramel poured over a thick salt block will cool and set much faster than on a baking sheet. Cool chocolate and caramels even faster by chilling the block slightly in the refrigerator or freezer before using it.

BAKED APPLES FILLED
WITH BROWN SUGAR STREUSEL

This dessert has all the flavors of apple pie. Add a little ice cream or whipped cream when serving and you'll hardly know the difference. The apples slowly steam on the salt block, becoming sweeter as they release their liquid. Take this dessert over the top—and into adults-only territory—with a splash of bourbon or Calvados when serving.

SERVES 4

PREP TIME: 10 MINUTES,
PLUS 25 MINUTES TO HEAT
THE SALT BLOCK

COOK TIME: 30 MINUTES

Canola oil

4 crisp apples, such as Gala, Braeburn, Honeycrisp, or Jonagold, halved lengthwise

2 tablespoons unsalted butter, melted

½ cup brown sugar

½ cup all-purpose flour

¼ teaspoon ground cinnamon

1. Preheat the oven to 350°F. Slowly heat the salt block on the stovetop to medium-high heat, about 25 minutes.

2. Once the salt block is hot, lightly oil the surface and place the apples on it, cut-side down. Place the block on the center rack in the oven.

3. While the apples are baking, make the streusel. In a large bowl, combine the melted butter and brown sugar. Add the flour and cinnamon and mix until the streusel is coarse and crumbly.

4. Remove the apples from the oven when they are soft and tender, about 30 minutes. Scoop the core out of the apples, fill the center of each with the streusel, and serve.

TIP Crisp apples are key to this recipe—avoid mealy apples.

PEANUT BUTTER COOKIES

There's something about peanut butter that just begs for salt. Baking these cookies on the salt block allows the dough to absorb a little extra seasoning. The cookies become slightly crisp from the radiant heat of the block but stay soft inside. Eat them with Salt Cup Chocolate Milk (page 157) for an extra special treat.

MAKES 24 COOKIES

PREP TIME: 20 MINUTES,
PLUS 25 MINUTES TO HEAT
THE SALT BLOCK

COOK TIME: 10 MINUTES

1 cup (2 sticks) unsalted butter, at room temperature

1 cup brown sugar

½ cup crunchy peanut butter

1 egg

1¼ cups all-purpose flour

1 teaspoon baking soda

½ teaspoon baking powder

Canola oil, for coating the block

1. Preheat the oven to 375°F. Slowly heat the salt block on the stovetop to medium-high heat, about 25 minutes. Once both are hot, place the salt block on the center rack in the oven.

2. In a large mixing bowl, cream together the butter and brown sugar, about 3 minutes. Mix in the peanut butter, then add the egg, and continue mixing until creamy.

3. Sift the flour, baking soda, and baking power into a medium bowl. Add this dry mixture to the mixing bowl and mix just until the flour is evenly incorporated; do not overmix.

4. Lightly oil the surface of the salt block. Roll the cookie dough into balls no larger than 1½ inches in diameter. Place the dough balls on the salt block and flatten each with the back of a fork. Bake until the bottom and edges begin to brown, 8 to 10 minutes. Serve warm.

TIP Use leftover cookies to make ice cream sandwiches: Place a scoop of vanilla ice cream between two cookies and gently press the cookies together. Wrap the sandwiches in plastic wrap and freeze for later.

SMASHED SALTED CARAMEL ICE CREAM

This dessert is not only a crowd pleaser but also equally fun for both kids and adults to make. Since the salt block isn't hot, this is a great way to get your kids involved without the concern of anyone getting burned. I like to store a salt block in my freezer so I'm always ready to make this treat.

SERVES 4

PREP TIME: 25 TO 30 MINUTES, PLUS OVERNIGHT TO CHILL THE SALT BLOCK

1 pint favorite ice cream

⅓ cup caramel sauce

Sea salt (optional)

1. Chill a salt block in the freezer overnight.

2. Temper the ice cream by placing it in the refrigerator for 20 minutes to soften slightly.

3. Place the frozen salt block on the counter with a kitchen towel underneath. Scoop the ice cream onto the salt block and drizzle the caramel sauce over it. Use two wooden spoons to smash and mix the ice cream and caramel together. Sprinkle the ice cream with some sea salt, if desired.

4. Serve this straight from the salt block or scoop it into cones.

TIP The flavoring combinations here are endless, so get creative. Try mixing in a chopped candy bar, crushed cookies, diced fresh fruit, or anything that strikes your fancy.

BITTERSWEET CHOCOLATE CIGARS

Who doesn't love chocolate? Here, the salt block cools the chocolate quickly, forming a thin sheet that will make the curls or cigars. Use a quality chocolate with a high cocoa percentage. Chocolate is mostly sugar and fat and contains little moisture, so it absorbs very little salt from the block, which is why this recipe calls for a little flaked salt to be added before the chocolate fully cools, to give a salty punch.

MAKES ABOUT 24 CIGARS

PREP TIME: 20 MINUTES,
PLUS 2 HOURS TO CHILL
THE SALT BLOCK

4 ounces bittersweet chocolate

1 tablespoon heavy
(whipping) cream

1 tablespoon finishing salt, such
as Maldon or fleur de sel

1. Refrigerate the salt block for 2 to 3 hours or overnight.

2. Using a double boiler or a heat-safe bowl placed over a pot of boiling water, gently heat the chocolate. Once it is melted, remove the pan or bowl from the heat and stir in the cream.

3. Remove the salt block from the refrigerator. Pour the chocolate onto the salt block and use an offset spatula to spread it very thinly across the surface. Sprinkle the salt evenly over the chocolate.

4. Once the chocolate has cooled, use a metal bench scraper or a knife to form curls: Place the scraper at a 45-degree angle to the salt block and push it away from you against the salt block so that the chocolate curls on itself, forming a tube. Repeat this process with the remaining chocolate. Wrap and refrigerate the cigars until you're ready to use them to garnish a dessert.

TIP Since this recipe doesn't require much chocolate, don't skimp—use the best quality you can. The curls don't have to be perfect. They still make a great garnish and taste delicious.

SALTED CARAMELS

Caramels are often made on marble slabs, which absorb the heat from the molten liquid and cool the caramel quickly. A salt block will do the same job. Placing two or more salt blocks next to each other gives you more surface area to work with and reduces the risk of the caramel spilling over the sides.

**MAKES ABOUT
60 CANDIES**

PREP TIME: 45 MINUTES,
PLUS 3 HOURS TO CHILL
THE SALT BLOCKS

COOK TIME: 20 MINUTES

1 ½ cups heavy
(whipping) cream

7 tablespoons unsalted butter

2 ¼ cups sugar

⅓ cup corn syrup

¼ cup water

Canola oil, for coating the blocks

Finishing salt, such as Maldon or
fleur de sel

1. Chill two salt blocks in the freezer for at least 3 hours or overnight.

2. Bring the cream and butter to a boil in a small saucepan. Remove the pan from the heat and set it aside.

3. Bring the sugar, corn syrup, and water to a boil in a medium-size saucepan. Gently swirl the pan to help dissolve the sugar, but do not stir it. If there are any sugar crystals stuck to the sides of the pan, dissolve them by brushing the sides with a wet pastry brush (these sugar crystals can disrupt the caramelization). Boil the mixture just until the liquid at the edges of the pan begins to change color.

4. Reduce the heat to low and swirl the saucepan to mix the caramel. When the caramel is a light amber color, take the pan off the heat and stir in the cream mixture with a wooden spoon or spatula. Caution: The caramel will bubble and may splatter. Return the pan to the heat and gently cook the caramel, stirring frequently, until the temperature registers 250°F on a candy thermometer, about 10 minutes.

5. Place the chilled salt blocks next to each other on the counter and lightly oil their surfaces. Slowly pour half of the caramel in the center of each block; use a rubber spatula to control the caramel so that it does not run off the sides. It will cool and set very quickly. Sprinkle the top of the caramel with finishing salt.

6. Once cooled and set, cut the caramel into 1-inch squares. Wrap each piece in a 3-inch square of parchment paper and twist the ends closed, or wrap them in plastic.

TIP Wrap aluminum foil around the sides of the salt block to form an elevated edge if you are worried about the caramel spilling over the sides.

CHOCOLATE CHIP COOKIES

This recipe has been adapted from The Local Butcher Shop in Berkeley, California. Their cookies are absolutely amazing. As owner Aaron Rocchino points out, each batch of lard behaves slightly differently so cookies will vary based on the lard you use. Lard is traditionally used in pies because it makes a rich, flaky crust. This recipe uses a mix of lard and butter so you get rich, savory cookies. Leaf lard is the highest-quality pork fat. Look for it at a local butcher shop that sources whole animals and sells freshly rendered lard.

MAKES 15 COOKIES

PREP TIME: 20 MINUTES, PLUS 2 HOURS TO CHILL

COOK TIME: 15 MINUTES

1 cup leaf lard, at room temperature

1 cup packed brown sugar

1 cup cane sugar

2 eggs

1 tablespoon pure vanilla extract

2 cups all-purpose flour

1 teaspoon baking soda

¾ cup bittersweet chocolate chips

1 teaspoon finishing salt, such as Maldon or fleur de sel

1. Cream the butter, lard, brown sugar, and cane sugar in a mixing bowl until light and fluffy, 2 to 4 minutes. Add the egg and vanilla and mix until evenly incorporated.

2. Sift the flour and baking soda into a bowl. Add the dry ingredients to the creamed butter until evenly incorporated, then add the chocolate chips. Mix until just combined; avoid overmixing.

3. Form the dough into a 1½-inch-diameter log, wrap with parchment paper, and refrigerate until fully chilled, about 2 hours.

4. Preheat the oven to 375°F and slowly heat the salt block on the stovetop to medium-high heat, about 25 minutes. Once both are hot, transfer the salt block to the center rack of the oven.

5. Slice the dough log into ½-inch-thick cookies and place them on the hot salt block. Sprinkle the cookies with the finishing salt. Bake until the bottoms are set and golden brown, 15 to 18 minutes. Cool slightly on a wire rack, or a room-temperature salt block, and serve.

TIP The dough can be made ahead of time and stored, tightly wrapped in plastic, in the freezer for up to a month before baking.

ROOT BEER FLOAT

The saltiness from the salt cup pairs surprisingly well with the sassafras flavor of the root beer. Other flavors work well, too. Try using orange soda for a Creamsicle-like drink, or use cola.

SERVES 4

PREP TIME: 5 MINUTES,
PLUS 2 HOURS TO CHILL
THE SALT CUPS

2 (12-ounce) bottles root beer, preferably Henry Weinhard's or Virgil's

1 pint vanilla ice cream

1. Chill four salt cups in the freezer for at least 2 hours or overnight.

2. Fill each salt cup halfway with root beer and add two scoops of ice cream to each cup. Serve with a spoon and straw.

TIP Using a straw reduces the saltiness since your lips will not absorb salt from contact with the rim of the salt cup.

QUICK BERRY TART

This is a great dessert that can be made in very little time if you have these few ingredients on hand. Prepare this tart while your dinner is in the final stages of cooking and bake it while you're enjoying your meal. The tart will be finished right around the time you're done eating. Serve it à la mode or with a little whipped cream.

SERVES 4

PREP TIME: 5 TO 10 MINUTES, PLUS 20 MINUTES TO HEAT THE SALT BLOCK

COOK TIME: 35 TO 45 MINUTES

3 cups fresh or frozen berries, tossed with vanilla extract or kirch

1 frozen pie crust, softened until pliable

1 tablespoon unsalted butter, melted

½ cup sugar

1. Preheat the oven to 400°F. Heat a salt block on the stovetop to medium heat, about 20 minutes. Once both are hot, transfer the salt block to the center rack of the oven.

2. Evenly scatter the berries in the pie crust. Fold the edges of the dough over the fruit to form a 1½-inch crust around the perimeter of the tart.

3. Brush the edges of the dough with the butter and shake the sugar evenly over the crust and fruit. Place the tart on the salt block and bake it until the bottom and edges of the tart are browned and the liquid from the fruit has reduced, 35 to 45 minutes. Let the tart cool slightly on a wire rack before serving.

TIP If you have the time or it's a special occasion, make your own tart dough. For a basic tart dough, combine 2 cups flour, 1 teaspoon salt, and 1 tablespoon sugar in the bowl of a stand mixer. Add 12 tablespoons unsalted butter cut into ½-inch cubes, and mix on low until the dough resembles coarse sand, about 1-2 minutes. Add ½ cup ice cold water and mix until combined, about 30 seconds. Divide the dough into 2 equal parts, and form into 1-inch thick disks. Wrap in plastic wrap and refrigerate for at least two hours before using.

HIBISCUS PANNA COTTA

If you have salt cups for drinking, odds are you are adventurous enough to try this salty dessert. The secret is to get both the salt cups and the panna cotta base very cold before combining. This will help set the panna cotta faster and reduce the contact time with the salt cup so that the dessert does not get too salty. As a general rule, the smaller the salt cup, the faster the panna cotta will set. I like to use cups that hold 4 ounces of liquid or less.

SERVES 6

PREP TIME: 30 MINUTES, PLUS OVERNIGHT TO CHILL THE SALT CUPS, AND 1 HOUR TO SET

COOK TIME: 10 MINUTES

2 tablespoons cold water

1 envelope unflavored gelatin (about 2½ teaspoons)

2 cups heavy (whipping) cream

1 cup whole milk

⅓ cup sugar

1 teaspoon pure vanilla extract

1 tablespoon ground hibiscus (see Tip)

1. Freeze 6 small (4-ounce) salt cups overnight.

2. Put the water in a small saucepan and sprinkle the gelatin evenly over the water. Set aside for 10 minutes. Gently heat the gelatin mixture over low heat until dissolved, stirring with a rubber spatula.

3. In a medium-size saucepan, heat the cream, milk, and sugar over medium heat until the sugar is completely dissolved. Remove from the heat. Add the gelatin and stir until the gelatin is completely dissolved. Strain the mixture through a fine-mesh sieve, stir in the vanilla and the hibiscus, and set aside to cool to room temperature.

4. Remove the salt cups from the freezer and pour the cooled panna cotta base into each cup. Place the salt cups in the refrigerator until the panna cotta is set, about 1 hour. Serve immediately.

TIP Hibiscus is an aromatic flower often used in teas. Look for it in the tea section of natural food stores. Feel free to use a blended hibiscus tea if you can't find the leaf in its pure form. Grind it into a powder with a spice grinder.

SALTED PEANUT BUTTER BANANA PANCAKES

This recipe makes for a truly decadent breakfast. Add bittersweet chocolate chips and toasted pecans and these pancakes quickly become dessert. Serve with unsweetened whipped cream to balance the sweetness of the pancakes.

MAKES 10 PANCAKES

PREP TIME: 15 MINUTES,
PLUS 25 MINUTES TO HEAT
THE SALT BLOCK

COOK TIME: 8 MINUTES

1½ cups all-purpose flour

2 tablespoons baking powder

1 overripe banana, mashed

⅓ cup peanut butter, smooth or crunchy

1 egg, beaten

1⅓ cups milk

2 tablespoons unsalted butter, melted

Canola oil, for coating the block

1. Slowly heat a salt block on the stovetop to medium-high heat, about 25 minutes.

2. In a medium bowl, combine the flour and baking powder. In another medium bowl, mix the banana, peanut butter, egg, milk, and butter until well combined. Add these wet ingredients to the flour and stir just until smooth. Do not overmix the batter.

3. Brush the hot salt block with oil and ladle ¼ cup of batter per pancake onto the salt block. Cook the pancakes until small bubbles appear on each pancake and their edges begin to brown, about 2 minutes. Flip the pancakes and continue cooking for 1 minute more. Serve immediately.

TIP If the peanut butter you use is particularly thick, you may need to increase the amount of milk you use. Likewise, if the peanut butter is on the runnier side, the amount of milk may need to be decreased.

CHAPTER TEN

DRINKS

There is something alluring about the challenge of finding a way to serve beverages in salt cups. The moment a liquid enters a salt cup it rapidly dissolves the salt, making the drink saltier with every passing moment. Drinks served in salt cups should be consumed quickly, as lingering over your drink may end in a less than pleasant beverage experience.

View a salt cup as a shape. A martini doesn't have to be served in a martini glass, but the shape of the martini glass adds to the overall enjoyment. The same can be said of salt cups: They may not be necessary to enjoy a beverage, but they add a fun element to drinking and, if nothing else, will spark a little conversation.

DRINK TIPS

➡ Chill both the salt cup and the beverage for as long as possible. Keeping the liquid and the salt cup cold reduces the rate of the salt dissolving into the drink. The lower temperature also reduces the perception of salt on your palate. Since the density of the cup is much greater than a normal glass, a salt cup will keep a beverage colder for longer, although you shouldn't take your time drinking these recipes.

➡ The longer your beverage sits in the cup, the saltier it will become. For this reason salt cups are great for taking shots, especially tequila. Keep this in mind and use salt cups for drinks that are meant to be enjoyed quickly.

➡ Choose cocktails and drinks that benefit from salt. The best example is a margarita, which is usually enjoyed with a salted rim. However, there are other drinks that work well, too. Sugar reduces the perception of salt, so serving a sweet beverage in a salt cup is a natural fit.

➡ Just as with food, salt enhances the flavor of beverages. Muddled cocktails work well in salt cups because the salt helps break down and extract flavors from citrus, mint, or whatever you're pounding in the bottom of the cup.

➡ Coat the rim of the cup with a flavored sugar or chocolate. By doing so you will greatly reduce the amount of salt absorbed by your lips while drinking.

TAMARIND AGUA FRESCA

Tamarind is a bitter seed popular in Latin American cuisines. Its bitterness can be an acquired taste, so you may want to increase the amount of sugar the first time you make this or if you are serving it to guests unfamiliar with tamarind. The salt from the cups helps soften the tamarind's bitterness.

SERVES 4

PREP TIME: 10 MINUTES, PLUS 3 HOURS TO STEEP, AND 1 HOUR TO CHILL THE SYRUP AND THE SALT CUPS

COOKING TIME: 5 MINUTES

4 to 5 ounces tamarind pods (see Tip)

2 cups water

½ cup sugar

Ice

Still or sparkling water

1. To make the tamarind syrup, first peel the tamarind pods and remove the seeds. Put the seeds in a medium-size saucepan, add the water, and bring to a boil. Boil for 3 minutes, then remove the pan from the heat. Set the pan aside and let the pods steep for 3 hours. Strain the liquid into another saucepan, pressing as much pulp through the sieve as possible. Add the sugar to the liquid and bring to a boil, stirring frequently, until the sugar dissolves. Transfer the syrup to a mason jar, tightly seal the jar, and refrigerate until completely chilled, about 1 hour. While the syrup is chilling, chill four salt cups in the refrigerator.

2. To assemble each drink, measure 1½ tablespoons tamarind syrup into each chilled salt cup. Add enough ice to fill the cup halfway, and top each off with sparkling or still water. Stir the contents to mix well and drink immediately.

TIP You can find whole tamarind pods in Latin American food markets, usually in the spice section.

SALTED CHERRY SHRUB

Shrubs are refreshing fruit-based vinegar drinks very similar to kombucha. Throughout history, when people couldn't be certain water was safe to drink, they drank vinegary shrubs. Serving shrubs in salt cups highlights the sweet and savory flavors of the drink. I suggest consulting a book on fermentation to best understand the safety components.

SERVES 4

PREP TIME: 10 MINUTES, PLUS
2 DAYS TO FERMENT AND 2 HOURS
TO CHILL THE SALT CUPS

1 cup fresh cherries, pitted
and halved

1 cup champagne vinegar

1 cup water

Ice

Sparkling water

1. Sterilize a 1-quart mason jar and its lid. Put the cherries in the jar.

2. In a small saucepan, heat the vinegar to 190°F. Pour it over the cherries. Use a clean cloth to wipe the rim of the jar clean before tightly sealing it with the lid. Store the jar in a cool, dark place. The vinegar is ready after 2 days.

3. Strain the vinegar through a large-mesh wire strainer, pushing as much cherry pulp through the strainer as possible. Transfer the vinegar to a clean mason jar, tightly seal the jar, and store it in the refrigerator until ready to use.

4. Chill four salt cups in the freezer for at least 2 hours or overnight. To make the shrubs, fill each chilled salt cup halfway with ice. Add 2 tablespoons of the vinegar to each cup and top each with the sparkling water. Stir and serve immediately.

TIP You can find a variety of drinking vinegars in many specialty food stores. Find others that you like and create your own specialty shrubs.

AROMATIC BLACK TEA OVER ICE

While you may think iced tea is best enjoyed on a hot day, this recipe is so tasty you'll want to serve it as an alcohol-free cocktail or aperitif all year round. You can make the tea in advance, but it is best when served as fresh as possible.

SERVES 4

PREP TIME: 2 HOURS,
PLUS 2 HOURS TO CHILL
THE SALT CUPS

1 quart water

2 tablespoons black tea leaves

1 tablespoon fennel
seed, cracked

1 whole clove

1 star anise pod

1 tablespoon dried orange peel

Ice

1. Chill four salt cups in the refrigerator for at least 2 hours or overnight.

2. In a large saucepan, bring the water to a boil. Remove the pan from the heat and add the tea. Steep for 3 minutes and strain. Add the fennel seed, clove, star anise, and orange peel. Steep the tea for 1 hour, then add 2 cups of ice to the pitcher to help cool the tea quickly (leaving the spices in the tea). Refrigerate the tea until it is cold, about 1 hour.

3. Fill each chilled salt cup halfway with ice. Pour the chilled tea over the ice. Drink immediately.

TIP Nearly any iced tea is delicious in a salt cup, so definitely experiment with other flavors.

SELTZER
WITH SALT-MUDDLED CITRUS

This refreshing drink is very quick and easy to make and, while this recipe calls for oranges, you can substitute nearly any type of citrus you have on hand. If you use a larger type of citrus, like grapefruit, the slices may need to be halved or quartered before being added to the salt cups to make it easier to muddle.

SERVES 4

PREP TIME: 5 MINUTES,
PLUS 2 HOURS TO CHILL
THE SALT CUPS

8 thin orange slices, unpeeled

Ice

Seltzer water

4 orange wedges, for garnish

1. Chill four salt cups in the freezer for at least 2 hours or overnight.

2. Place 2 orange slices in the bottom of each chilled salt cup. Muddle the slices by mashing them with a wooden spoon to break up the orange and release the juice.

3. Fill each salt cup halfway with ice. Add enough seltzer water to fill the cup, and garnish each with an orange wedge on the edge of the cup. Serve immediately.

TIP Muddling intensifies the citrus flavor and draws salt out of the cup. Don't be afraid to be aggressive when mashing the citrus. If you want your drink less salty, you can muddle the citrus in a bowl or mortar before adding it to the salt cup.

SALT CUP CHOCOLATE MILK

This is a good starter drink for kids or for anyone who is more sensitive to salt. By coating the rim of the salt cup with chocolate, the drink takes on less salt as you sip it. I like this best with just milk, but you can stir in some chocolate syrup for an especially sweet and decadent drink.

SERVES 4

PREP TIME: 10 MINUTES, PLUS 2 HOURS TO CHILL THE SALT CUPS

4 ounces bittersweet chocolate, melted

Whole milk

1. Chill four salt cups in the freezer for at least 2 hours or overnight.

2. Dip the top half of each chilled salt cup rim in the warm chocolate and set it on the counter. The chocolate will set immediately on the cold rim. Fill each cup with cold whole milk. Drink immediately.

TIP I use this same chocolate rim method when serving desserts in salt cups. Add a scoop of ice cream and some fresh fruit for an easy dessert that is sure to impress.

ULTIMATE MARGARITA

The salt from the cup means you don't need to salt the rim of this margarita. Skip the margarita mixer and use fresh limes for a drink that is guaranteed to go down smooth.

MAKES 4 DRINKS

PREP TIME: 10 MINUTES, PLUS 2 HOURS TO CHILL THE SALT CUPS

4 ounces tequila

4 ounces freshly squeezed lime juice

4 ounces Grand Mariner

Ice

4 lime wedges, for garnish

1. Chill four salt cups in the freezer for at least 2 hours or overnight.

2. In a small pitcher, combine the tequila, lime juice, and triple sec. Add 2 cups of ice to the pitcher and stir the margarita for about 30 seconds.

3. Fill each salt cup halfway with ice and pour the margarita over the ice. Garnish each cup rim with a lime wedge and serve immediately.

TIP If you like a sweeter margarita, run a lime wedge around the rim of the salt cup and then dip it in sugar.

OLD FASHIONED
WITH SALT-MUDDLED ORANGE

The old fashioned is a classic cocktail, and here it gets a twist from the salt glass. The orange takes on salt during the muddling, so make sure not to overdo it. Grab your favorite bottle of bourbon and serve this during cocktail hour or enjoy it with a Seared Rib Eye with Salt Block Green Peppercorn Sauce (page 71) at dinner.

SERVES 4

PREP TIME: 5 TO 10 MINUTES, PLUS 2 HOURS TO CHILL THE SALT CUPS

8 dashes Angostura bitters, divided

4 sugar cubes, divided

8 orange slices, unpeeled, divided

6 ounces bourbon, divided

Club soda

4 maraschino cherries, for garnish

1. Chill four salt cups in the freezer for at least 2 hours or overnight.

2. Add 2 dashes of bitters, 1 sugar cube, and 1 orange slice to each chilled salt cup and muddle with the handle of a wooden spoon.

3. Remove the orange rind from the cups and add 1½ ounces of bourbon to each. Fill each salt cup halfway with ice and then fill each cup with club soda. Garnish each cup with a maraschino cherry and another orange slice and serve.

TIP Some may prefer the orange only as a garnish, so feel free to muddle only the bitters and sugar cube. You can also add a little simple syrup to the pitcher before stirring.

PISCO SOUR

While travelling in Peru, I drank more pisco sours than I could possibly count. They are refreshing and taste great alone or served with food. Serve them with Sea Bass Ceviche with Red Onion and Corn (page 46) in the summer when dining al fresco—it's just the thing to beat the summer heat.

SERVES 4

PREP TIME: 10 MINUTES, PLUS 2 HOURS TO CHILL THE SALT CUPS

8 ounces pisco, such as BarSol Primero Quebranta, divided

4 ounces freshly squeezed lime juice, divided

2 ounces simple syrup, divided

4 egg whites, divided

Ice

Angostura bitters, for garnish

1. Chill four salt cups in the freezer for at least 2 hours or overnight.

2. Combine 4 ounces of pisco, 2 ounces of lime juice, 1 ounce of simple syrup, and 2 egg whites in a cocktail shaker. Cover the shaker and shake vigorously for 45 seconds. Add 3 to 5 ice cubes to the shaker and shake vigorously for another 45 seconds.

3. Fill two chilled salt cups halfway with ice and strain the pisco sour into the cups through a fine-mesh strainer. Garnish each cup with three dots of the bitters in the form of a triangle. Repeat this process to make another two drinks.

TIP This dish absolutely must have the raw egg whites, so if you're nervous about drinking them, this cocktail isn't for you.

AMARETTO SOUR

This is my favorite cocktail, period. It is inspired by the amaretto sour made at Clyde Common in Portland, Oregon. A better amaretto sour cannot be had, so make sure to visit the bar if you're in Portland, although it won't be served in a salt cup.

SERVES 2

PREP TIME: 10 MINUTES,
PLUS 2 HOURS TO CHILL
THE SALT CUPS

3 ounces amaretto

3 ounces bourbon or 1½ ounces cask-proof bourbon

2 ounces freshly squeezed lemon juice

2 teaspoons simple syrup

1 egg white

Ice

2 (1-inch-wide) strips lemon peel, for garnish

Maraschino cherries, for garnish

1. Chill the salt cups in the freezer for at least 2 hours or overnight.

2. Combine the amaretto, bourbon, lemon juice, simple syrup, and egg white in a cocktail shaker. Cover the shaker and shake it vigorously for 30 seconds. Add ice to the shaker and shake vigorously for another 30 seconds.

3. Strain the amaretto sour through a fine-mesh sieve into two chilled salt cups. Gently tap each cup on the counter to settle the foam and remove the larger air bubbles. Garnish each drink by twisting the lemon strips and placing one in each cup. Add a cherry on top of each lemon strip and serve.

TIP Cask-proof bourbon is the purest bourbon around. It is bottled without the addition of water, so it has a much higher alcohol content and is not overpowered by the sweetness of the amaretto.

MINT JULEP

The mint julep is a sweet Southern cocktail that is often served in a metal cup and sipped at horse races or other social activities. Here we stick to the classic recipe but use a salt cup, which cuts the sweetness a bit. The salt cup also helps bring out extra mint oil during the muddling process.

SERVES 2

PREP TIME: 10 MINUTES,
PLUS 2 HOURS TO CHILL
THE ICE CUPS

8 fresh mint leaves, divided

1½ ounces simple syrup

Ice

4 ounces bourbon, divided

Cold water

2 mint sprigs, for garnish

1. Chill two salt cups in the freezer for at least 2 hours or overnight.

2. Put 4 mint leaves and ¾ ounce of simple syrup in each chilled salt cup. Use a wooden spoon to muddle the leaves and syrup, which releases the oil in the mint. Fill each cup halfway with ice and then add 2 ounces of bourbon to each cup. Top off each cup with cold water and stir.

3. Garnish each cup with a sprig of fresh mint and drink immediately.

TIP This drink is meant to be served in an 8- or 10-ounce highball glass, so you may need to rescale the ingredients depending on the size of your salt cups.

STRAWBERRY DAIQUIRI
WITH A BASIL-SUGAR RIM

With the beginning of summer comes strawberries, and as the season continues I always find that I have plenty of overripe strawberries that need to be cooked or puréed. This drink is the perfect use for overripe, soft strawberries, as their high sugar content will be contrasted with the salt from the cup. Use the strawberries before they go bad or remove the stems and freeze them on a sheet tray. Once frozen, store them in a resealable bag for future use. This makes it super easy to use the exact number of strawberries for your daiquiri and ensure it will be icy cold and delicious.

SERVES 2

PREP TIME: 20 MINUTES,
PLUS OVERNIGHT TO DRY
THE BASIL SUGAR AND
CHILL THE SALT CUPS

1 cup chopped fresh basil leaves

1 cup plus 2 tablespoons
sugar, divided

1 cup crushed ice

12 very large strawberries

4 ounces white rum

1 ounce freshly squeezed
lime juice

1 lime wedge

1. To make the basil sugar for the rim, combine the basil and 1 cup of sugar in a medium bowl and stir to mix. Spread the sugared basil on a sheet tray that has enough surface area to allow the basil to dry. Leave the sheet tray out overnight, uncovered, to dry. Store the basil sugar in a tightly sealed container at room temperature.

2. Chill the salt cups in the freezer for at least 2 hours or overnight.

3. Combine the crushed ice, strawberries, rum, lime juice, and the remaining 2 tablespoons of sugar in a blender. Blend until smooth. If the purée seems too thick, add a little water to reach your preferred consistency.

4. Run the lime wedge around the rims of the chilled salt cups and dip the rims into the basil sugar. Divide the daiquiri between the two cups and serve immediately.

TIP Other fruits work well with this daiquiri, too. Try fresh, very ripe mango for a tropical twist or peaches to beat the summer heat. I don't recommend berries such as blackberries and raspberries.

MEASUREMENT CONVERSIONS

VOLUME EQUIVALENTS (LIQUID)

US STANDARD	US STANDARD (OUNCES)	METRIC (APPROXIMATE)
2 tablespoons	1 fl. oz.	30 mL
¼ cup	2 fl. oz.	60 mL
½ cup	4 fl. oz.	120 mL
1 cup	8 fl. oz.	240 mL
1½ cups	12 fl. oz.	355 mL
2 cups or 1 pint	16 fl. oz.	475 mL
4 cups or 1 quart	32 fl. oz.	1 L
1 gallon	128 fl. oz.	4 L

OVEN TEMPERATURES

FAHRENHEIT (F)	CELSIUS (C) (APPROXIMATE)
250°	120°
300°	150°
325°	165°
350°	180°
375°	190°
400°	200°
425°	220°
450°	230°

VOLUME EQUIVALENTS (DRY)

US STANDARD	METRIC (APPROXIMATE)
⅛ teaspoon	0.5 mL
¼ teaspoon	1 mL
½ teaspoon	2 mL
¾ teaspoon	4 mL
1 teaspoon	5 mL
1 tablespoon	15 mL
¼ cup	59 mL
⅓ cup	79 mL
½ cup	118 mL
⅔ cup	156 mL
¾ cup	177 mL
1 cup	235 mL
2 cups or 1 pint	475 mL
3 cups	700 mL
4 cups or 1 quart	1 L

WEIGHT EQUIVALENTS

US STANDARD	METRIC (APPROXIMATE)
½ ounce	15 g
1 ounce	30 g
2 ounces	60 g
4 ounces	115 g
8 ounces	225 g
12 ounces	340 g
16 ounces or 1 pound	455 g

RESOURCES

AMAZON

Amazon carries a variety of discounted salt block products, many available with free shipping for Amazon Prime members.
www.amazon.com

CRATE & BARREL

National retailer carrying salt blocks and related products.
www.crateandbarrel.com
800-967-6696

THE MEADOW

With retail locations in Portland, Oregon and New York City as well as an online shop, The Meadow sells a large variety of Himalayan salt blocks, bowls, cups and related products.
www.themeadow.com
503-288-4633

SUR LA TABLE

National retailer carrying salt blocks and related products.
www.surlatable.com
800-243-0852

WILLIAMS-SONOMA

National retailer carrying salt blocks and related products.
www.williams-sonoma.com
877-812-6235

RECIPE INDEX

INDEX

ACKNOWLEDGMENTS

Thanks to the wonderful people at Callisto Media, especially Talia Platz, Frances Baca, and Meg Woodcheke.

Thanks to Anthony Tassinello for all his support and sorting through every fish at Tokyo Fish Market to find the perfect sea bream.

Thanks to Aaron and Monica Rocchino and The Local Butcher Shop.

Thanks to all the extraordinary people who made the photo shoot possible: Leigh Wells for sharing her studio and home, Joy Brace for the beautiful apron. Thanks to Kelly Ishikawa, Rod Hipskind and Grant Stiles for the lovely photography.

Thanks to my favorite people to cook for: my wife Carrie and daughters Elsa and Ava.

Thanks to all the talented people I've worked with and learned from over the years, but especially those at Chez Panisse who began as coworkers and have become family.

And finally thanks to David Tanis, who hired me on a whim, introducing me to Alice Waters and Chez Panisse. I am eternally grateful.

ABOUT THE AUTHOR

RYAN CHILDS is a professional chef, recipe developer, and food writer. He is a graduate of the Le Cordon Bleu College of Culinary Arts in San Francisco. His cooking is most influenced by his years working at Chez Panisse in Berkeley, California. He has also worked as a chef at Aqua, Gary Danko, flour + water, and Cotogna. When not in the kitchen, Ryan can be found exploring the Pacific Northwest and foraging mushrooms. He lives in Portland, Oregon, with his wife and two daughters.